PONS

# Übungsbuch zum Schulbuch

Passend für:
- Camden Town 2
- English G 21 A2
- English G access 2
- Green Line 2 (Ausgabe 2006)
- Green Line 2 (Ausgabe 2015)

# Englisch 2

Gymnasium
6. Klasse

Sarah Nowotny

**PONS GmbH**
Stuttgart

**PONS**

**Übungsbuch zum Schulbuch**
**ENGLISCH 2**
**Gymnasium 6. Klasse**

von
Sarah Nowotny

**Die Audiodateien zu diesem Titel findest du unter**
**www.pons.de/übungsbuch-zum-schulbuch-englisch2**
**oder scanne den QR-Code.**

Auflage A1 5 4 3 2 1 / 2019 2018 2017 2016



**Redaktion:** PONS Lernhilfen
**Logoentwurf:** Erwin Poell, Heidelberg
**Logoüberarbeitung:** Sabine Redling, Heidelberg
**Umschlagfoto:** Fotolia, New York (BillionPhotos.com)
**Einbandgestaltung:** Sabine Kaufmann, Stuttgart
**Satz:** DTP-studio Andrea Eckhardt, Göppingen
**Druck und Bindung:** Gebr. Geiselberger GmbH, Altötting

Printed in Germany
**ISBN 978-3-12-562523-5**

# Vorwort: Alles ganz einfach – the easy way!

In diesem Übungsbuch findest du:

## Grammatik

Alle Grammatikthemen deiner Klasse findest du schnell, wenn du im Inhaltsverzeichnis ab Seite 4 suchst. Schlage die angegebene Seite dieses Übungsbuches auf – du findest hier viele Übungen mit unterschiedlichem Schwierigkeitsgrad. Auf den Seiten gleich nach den Übungen stehen die Lösungen.

## Textverständnis

Im zweiten Buchteil findest du Übungen zu Themen, die in deiner Klassenstufe behandelt werden. Es gibt Übungen zum

- Hörverstehen
- Schreiben von eigenen Texten
- Leseverstehen
- Sprachmittlung (Mediation)

**Passend zum**
## Schulbuch

Dieses Übungsbuch passt genau zu deinem Schulbuch. Suche dein eigenes Schulbuch auf den Seiten unseres Wegweisers – du kannst diese Seiten mit einem „Eselsohr" oder einem Lesezeichen markieren, um sie immer schnell wieder zu finden.
Dein ganz persönlicher Wegweiser zeigt dir immer genau an, auf welcher Seite dieses Übungsbuches du findest, was bei dir in der Schule gerade dran ist. Du findest jede Unit, alle Grammatikthemen, Wortschatzübungen und alle Themen, die ihr in der Schule behandelt. So kannst du alles wiederholen und bist immer gut vorbereitet.

**WEGWEISER**
**Passend für:**

# Inhaltsverzeichnis

# Inhaltsverzeichnis

# Inhaltsverzeichnis

# Inhaltsverzeichnis

## Textverständnis

## Unit 1 – Camden Town 2

**Grammatik**

**Wortschatz – Textverständnis**



## Unit 2 – Camden Town 2

**Grammatik**



**Wortschatz – Textverständnis**



## Unit 3 – Camden Town 2

**Grammatik**

## Unit 4 – Camden Town 2

**Grammatik**

## Unit 5 – Camden Town 2

### Grammatik



### Wortschatz – Textverständnis



## Unit 6 – Camden Town 2

### Grammatik



### Wortschatz – Textverständnis

## Unit 1 – English G 21 A2



## Unit 2 – English G 21 A2

## Unit 3 – English G 21 A2

**Grammatik**

## Unit 4 – English G 21 A2

## Unit 5 – English G 21 A2

### Grammatik



### Wortschatz – Textverständnis



## Unit 6 – English G 21 A2

### Grammatik

**Wortschatz – Textverständnis**

## Unit 1 – English G access 2

**Grammatik**

## Unit 3 – English G access 2

**Grammatik**





**Wortschatz – Textverständnis**



## Unit 4 – English G access 2

**Grammatik**

## Unit 5 – English G access 2

**Grammatik**

**Wortschatz – Textverständnis**



## Unit 6 – English G access 2



**Grammatik**



**Wortschatz – Textverständnis**

## Unit 1 – Green Line 2 (Ausgabe 2006)

### Grammatik



### Wortschatz – Textverständnis



## Unit 2 – Green Line 2 (Ausgabe 2006)

### Grammatik

**Wortschatz – Textverständnis**



## Unit 6 – Green Line 2 (Ausgabe 2006)

**Grammatik**



**Wortschatz – Textverständnis**

## Unit 7 – Green Line 2 (Ausgabe 2006)

**Grammatik**



**Wortschatz – Textverständnis**



## Trailer 1 – Green Line 2 (Ausgabe 2006)

**Grammatik**



**Wortschatz – Textverständnis**

## **Trailer 2 – Green Line 2** (Ausgabe 2006)

**Grammatik**



**Wortschatz – Textverständnis**





## **Trailer 3 – Green Line** (Ausgabe 2006)

**Grammatik**



**Wortschatz – Textverständnis**

## Unit 1 – Green Line 2 (Ausgabe 2015)

### Grammatik



### Wortschatz – Textverständnis



## Unit 2 – Green Line 2 (Ausgabe 2015)

### Grammatik

**Wortschatz – Textverständnis**



## Unit 3 – Green Line 2 (Ausgabe 2015)

**Grammatik**



**Wortschatz – Textverständnis**



## Unit 4 – Green Line 2 (Ausgabe 2015)

**Grammatik**



**Wortschatz – Textverständnis**

## **Unit 5 – Green Line 2** (Ausgabe 2015)

**Grammatik**



**Wortschatz – Textverständnis**



## **Unit 6 – Green Line 2** (Ausgabe 2015)

**Grammatik**



**Wortschatz – Textverständnis**

# GRAMMATIK

# Die einfache Form der Gegenwart (*The simple present*)

## 1 Aussagesätze (*Statements*)

●○○ 1. Finde das richtige Verb für die Lücken. → Lösung S. 42

a) Those shoes ________ expensive.

b) I ________ a lot of texts.

c) Our dog ________ in a basket.

d) You ________ too much cola!

●○○ 2. Ergänze *-s* oder *-es*, falls nötig. → Lösung S. 42

a) It often rain ________ in Wales.

b) I like ________ tennis but I can't play it.

c) Jim and Patrick go ________ to the same school.

d) Gary watch ________ too much TV!

e) Our teacher never give ________ us homework on Fridays.

f) You talk ________ too much. Please be quiet.

g) Marie wash ________ her hair in the evening.

h) The cat eat ________ a lot of fish.

●○○ 3. Fülle die Lücken. Manchmal brauchst du auch die verneinte Form des Verbs. → Lösung S. 42

a) Sorry, I ________ (*know*) the answer.

b) Sally ________________ (*eat*) a lot of curry. It's her favourite food.

c) We ________________ (*live*) in Acorn Street now. We live in Fir Road.

d) They ________________ (*play*) football every Friday, even in the rain!

e) My dad ________________ (*remember*) his password, so he can't check his e-mail today.

f) I ________________ (*like*) homework. It's so boring!

g) Tina ________________ (*read*) a lot of books. It's her hobby.

●●○ 4. Schreibe aus den Wörtern richtige Sätze. → Lösung S. 42

a) lives / near / school / our / Ron

______________________________________________

b) fish / eat / I / don't

______________________________________________

c) remembers / my / Lucy / always / birthday

______________________________________________

d) don't / English / we / today / lesson / an / have

______________________________________________

e) school / in / choir / sings / the / Lisa

______________________________________________

f) speak / French / doesn't / Jamie

______________________________________________

## 2 Fragen und Kurzantworten (*Questions and short answers*)

●○○ 1. Schreibe Fragen und Kurzantworten mit den Informationen aus der Tabelle. → Lösung S. 42

| | Simon | Anna and Eddie |
|---|---|---|
| play the guitar | ✓ | ✗ |
| go to school by bus | ✓ | ✗ |
| enjoy scary films | ✗ | ✓ |
| have a dog | ✓ | ✗ |

a) Does Simon play the guitar? – Yes, he does.

b) ______

c) ______

d) ______

e) ______

f) ______

g) ______

h) ______

●○○ 2. Antworte mit einer Kurzantwort. → Lösung S. 42

a) Do you need any help? – No, ______ .

b) Does your sister play ice-hockey? – Yes, ______ .

c) Do your parents come from Germany? – No, ______ .

d) Do we have any homework today? – Yes, ______ .

e) Does Peter live near you? – No, ______ .

## 3 Fragen mit Fragewörtern (*Questions with question words*)

●○○ 1. Füge das richtige Fragewort ein. → Lösung S. 42

how • what • when • where • which • who

a) ______________ time do you get up at the weekend?

b) ______________ does Mark live?

c) ______________ do you sit next to at school?

d) ______________ do they want to eat?

e) ______________ film do you want to see?

f) ______________ do you spell "beautiful"?

g) ______________ does the football match start?

h) ______________ do we need to go?

●●○ 2. Stelle die Frage, die zur Antwort passt. Frage dabei nach den schräg gedruckten Satzteilen. → Lösung S. 42

a) The film starts *at 5 o'clock*.

What time does the film start?

b) My mum works *in a bank*.

______________________________

c) That girl over there is *my sister*.

______________________________

d) „Kopfhörer" means "*headphones*" in English.

______________________________

e) The maths test is *on Wednesday*.

______________________________

## 4 Gemischte Formen (*Mixed forms*)

●○○ 1. Verbinde die beiden passenden Satzteile. → Lösung S. 43

| | |
|---|---|
| a) Frannie never listens | in ghosts. |
| b) These cookies taste | to me. |
| c) Please don't forget | a film at the weekend. |
| d) Jack usually does | really bad jokes. |
| e) They often watch | a text. |
| f) I don't believe | really good! |
| g) My dad always tells | his homework in the afternoon. |
| h) Mike sometimes sends me | Auntie Kitty's birthday! |

●○○ 2. Hier haben sich Fehler eingeschlichen.
Schreibe den Satz richtig auf. → Lösung S. 43

a) Martin often go to the cinema.

______________________________

b) "Do you like horses?" – "Yes, I like."

______________________________

c) I watch sometimes TV before breakfast.

______________________________

d) What time leaves the train?

______________________________

e) Ben don't ride his bike in winter.

______________________________

f) They plays basketball every Thursday.

______________________________

●●○ 3. Ergänze den Text mit den angegebenen Verben – aber achte dabei auf die richtige Verbform. → Lösung S. 43

be • be • chat • do • finish • get • not/get • go • live • meet • not/see • start

Sophie ______________ from Manchester, but now she and her parents ______________ in Germany. Some things ______________ quite different now. For example, Sophie ______________ up at half past seven now. Her new school ______________ at 8 o'clock, so now she ______________ up at half past six. That's early! But Sophie and her friends ______________ school earlier than in England, too: they usually ______________ home at 1 o'clock. After lunch, Sophie ______________ her homework. She ______________ her friends every afternoon. Sometimes they ______________ in the town centre, but they often just ______________ online.

●●○ 4. Wie sagt man das auf Englisch? → Lösung S. 43

a) Mein Bruder trinkt viel Kaffee.

______________________________________________

b) Siehst du jeden Abend fern?

______________________________________________

c) Dan arbeitet nicht in York.

______________________________________________

d) Die Kinder essen Kartoffelchips nach der Schule.

______________________________________________

e) Brauchen wir heute unsere Englischbücher?

______________________________________________

## 1 Aussagesätze (*Statements*)

Übungen ab S. 36

1. a) Those shoes **are** expensive. b) I **send** a lot of texts. c) Our dog **sleeps** in a basket. d) You **drink** too much cola!

2. a) It often **rains** in Wales. b) I **like** tennis but I can't play it. c) Jim and Patrick **go** to the same school. d) Gary **watches** too much TV ! e) Our teacher never **gives** us homework on Fridays. f) You **talk** too much. Please be quiet. g) Marie **washes** her hair in the evening. g) The cat **eats** a lot of fish.

3. a) Sorry, I **don't know** the answer. b) Sally **eats** a lot of curry. It's her favourite food. c) We **don't live** in Acorn Street now. We live in Fir Road. d) They **play** football every Friday, even in the rain! e) My dad **doesn't remember** his password, so he can't check his e-mail today. f) I **don't like** homework. It's so boring! g) Tina **reads** a lot of books. It's her hobby.

4. a) Ron lives near our school. b) I don't eat fish. c) Lucy always remembers my birthday. d) We don't have an English lesson today. e) Lisa sings in the school choir. f) Jamie doesn't speak French.

## 2 Fragen und Kurzantworten (*Questions and short answers*)

Übungen ab S. 38

1. b) Do Anna and Eddie play the guitar? – No, they don't. c) Does Simon go to school by bus? – Yes, he does. d) Do Anna and Eddie go to school by bus? – No, they don't. e) Does Simon enjoy scary films? – No, he doesn't. f) Do Anna and Eddie enjoy scary films? – Yes, they do. g) Does Simon have a dog? – Yes, he does. h) Do Anna and Eddie have a dog? – No, they don't.

2. a) No, I don't. b) Yes, she does. c) No, they don't. d) Yes, we do. e) No, he doesn't.

## 3 Fragen mit Fragewörtern (*Questions with question words*)

Übungen ab S. 39

1. a) **What** time do you get up at the weekend? b) **Where** does Mark live? c) **Who** do you sit next to at school? d) **What** do they want to eat? e) **Which** film do you want to see? f) **How** do you spell "beautiful"? g) **When** does the football match start? h) **Where** do we need to go?

2. b) Where does your mum work? c) Who is that girl over there? d) What does "Kopfhörer" mean in English? e) When is the maths test?

## 4 Gemischte Formen (*Mixed forms*)

→ Übungen ab S. 40

1. b) These cookies taste really good! c) Please don't forget Auntie Kitty's birthday! d) Jack usually does his homework in the afternoon. e) They often watch a film at the weekend. f) I don't believe in ghosts. g) My dad always tells really bad jokes. h) Mike sometimes sends me a text.

2. a) Martin often **goes** to the cinema. b) "Yes, I **do**." c) I **sometimes watch** TV before breakfast. d) What time **does** the train **leave**? e) Ben **doesn't** ride his bike in winter. f) They **play** basketball every Thursday.

3. Sophie **is** from Manchester, but now she and her parents **live** in Germany. Some things **are** quite different now. For example, Sophie **doesn't get** up at half past seven now. Her new school **starts** at 8 o'clock, so now she **gets** up at half past six. That's early! But Sophie and her friends **finish** school earlier than in England, too: they usually **go** home at 1 o'clock. After lunch, Sophie **does** her homework. She **doesn't see** her friends every afternoon. Sometimes they **meet** in the town centre, but they often just **chat** online.

4. a) My brother drinks a lot of coffee. b) Do you watch TV every evening? c) Dan doesn't work in York. d) The children eat crisps after school. e) Do we need our English books today?

# Die einfache Form der Vergangenheit (*The simple past*)

## 1 Aussprache und Schreibung (*Pronunciation and spelling*)

●○○ 1. Bilde die Vergangenheitsformen der Verben. Welche Laute hörst du am Ende? Trage in die richtige Spalte ein. → Lösung S. 55

agree • arrive • ask • call • check • climb • cook • correct • dance • drop • enjoy • finish • follow • help • invite • like • need • score • shout • start • stop • visit • wait • want

| [d] | [t] | [ɪd] |
|---|---|---|
| agreed | | |
| | | |
| | | |
| | | |
| | | |
| | | |
| | | |
| | | |

●○○ 2. Setze die Verben in die einfache Vergangenheit. Achte dabei auf mögliche Besonderheiten. → Lösung S. 55

a) play ______________ b) end ______________

c) change ______________ d) shop ______________

e) carry ______________ f) need ______________

g) stop ______________ h) try ______________

i) believe ______________ j) laugh ______________

k) stay ______________ l) phone ______________

## 2 Regelmäßige Verben (*Regular verbs*)

●○○ 1. Füge das richtige Verb in die Lücken ein.
Benutze dabei die einfache Vergangenheit. → Lösung S. 55

ask • follow • help • listen • look • need •
open • score • start • taste • visit

a) It was hot in the room, so I ________________ the window.

b) My grandparents ________________ us last weekend.

c) The fire ________________ in the kitchen.

d) We ________________ Annie get everything ready for the party.

e) A little white cat ________________ us all the way home.

f) At the last minute, Tony ________________ the winning goal!

g) They ________________ to the beautiful music.

h) Our teacher ________________ us a lot of questions.

i) Tom ________________ money, so he ________________ for a job.

j) The curry ________________ really spicy!

●○○ 2. Ergänze die Sätze mit den angegebenen Verben in der Vergangenheit – manche Verben musst du verneinen. → Lösung S. 55

a) We ________________ (wait) for Emma for a long time
but she ________________ (arrive).

b) The test was very hard. I ________________ (understand)
most of the questions.

c) These shoes were quite cheap. They ________________ (cost) much.

d) I really ________________ (enjoy) the party but I ________________
(like) the food.

e) We ________________ (dance) all night at Charlie's party.

●○○ 3. Sortiere die Wörter zu einem Satz mit richtiger englischer Wortstellung.

→ Lösung S. 55

a) cooked / Sandy / for / everyone / dinner

______________________________

b) bed / children / the / on / jumped / the

______________________________

c) didn't / his / clean / room / Samuel

______________________________

d) walked / in / dog / Pete / the / park / his

______________________________

e) my / laugh / at / joke / didn't / they

______________________________

f) match / the / trained / for / team / the / hard

______________________________

●○○ 4. Kreuze die Verbform an, die in die Lücke gehört.

→ Lösung S. 55

a) Clara ______________ in the match yesterday.

☐ played not ☐ didn't play

b) The train ______________ at the station.

☐ stopped ☐ stoped

c) My brother ______________ me with my homework.

☐ didn't helped ☐ didn't help

d) Mum ______________ the baby upstairs.

☐ carried ☐ carryed

## 3 Die einfache Vergangenheit von *to be* (*The simple past of "to be"*)

●○○ 1. Setze die einfache Vergangenheit von *to be* in Lücken ein. Du brauchst dafür *was* oder *were*.

→ Lösung S. 56

a) Our last tennis match ______________ very exciting!

b) Picasso ______________ a famous painter.

c) Liam and Sammy ______________ at the cinema last weekend.

d) It ______________ very hot last summer.

●○○ 2. Ergänze die verneinte Form von *to be* wie in dem Beispiel.

→ Lösung S. 56

a) I *wasn't* at home. I was in the park.

b) They ______________ from Spain. They were from Portugal.

c) You ______________ right. You were wrong.

d) Rebecca ______________ at the party. She was on holiday.

e) The film ______________ at 5 p.m. It was at 6 p.m.

f) We ______________ at the train station. We were at the bus station.

g) Her jacket ______________ red. It was black.

h) Paul and Andy ______________ at the pizzeria. They were at the café.

●○○ 3. Schreibe Fragen und ergänze dabei *was* oder *were*. → Lösung S. 56

a) you / at / Helen's / party

Were you at Helen's party?

b) the / test / easy

______________________________

c) that / your / sister

______________________________

d) your / parents / angry / with / you / last / night

______________________________

e) it / Tim's / birthday / yesterday

______________________________

f) the / flowers / for / your / mum

______________________________

●○○ 4. Schreibe Kurzantworten zu den Fragen. → Lösung S. 56

a) Was Matthew 12 on his last birthday? – Yes, ______________ .

b) Were the children in the garden? – No, ______________ .

c) Were you busy on Monday? – Yes, ______________ .

d) Was the weather nice yesterday? – No, ______________ .

e) Were your parents happy with their present? – Yes, ______________ .

f) Was Julia at school yesterday? – No, ______________ .

g) Was your laptop expensive? – Yes, ______________ .

h) Were the shops open at 10 o'clock last night? – No, ______________ .

## 4 Unregelmäßige Formen (*Irregular forms*)

●○○ 1. Diese Verben bilden die Vergangenheit unregelmäßig. Ergänze die Tabelle.

→ Lösung S. 56

| infinitive | simple past | infinitive | simple past |
|---|---|---|---|
| (to) break | | (to) buy | |
| (to) come | | (to) drink | |
| (to) eat | | (to) find | |
| (to) give | | (to) go | |
| (to) leave | | (to) meet | |
| (to) take | | (to) write | |
| (to) have | | (to) see | |
| (to) get | | (to) do | |
| (to) stand | | (to) read | |
| (to) swim | | (to) fall | |
| (to) think | | (to) make | |
| (to) know | | (to) sell | |

●○○ 2. Ergänze die Sätze mit Verben aus der Tabelle der Aufgabe 1 in der einfachen Vergangenheit.

→ Lösung S. 57

a) I once ______________ a very famous singer!

b) She ______________ some beautiful flowers for her mother.

c) Jake ______________ me his new phone number.

d) The skiing trip wasn't much fun. I ______________ my leg!

e) Jessie ______________ to the shopping centre to buy some new shoes.

f) Marc isn't here now. He ______________ ten minutes ago.

g) I ______________ this phone in the playground. Is it yours?

h) We were thirsty, so we ______________ some water.

●●○ 3. Ergänze das Kreuzworträtsel mit Vergangenheitsformen der angegebenen Verben.

→ Lösung S. 57

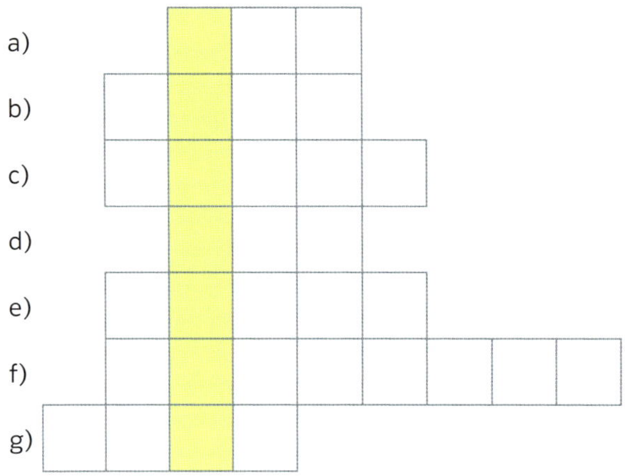


buy • do • put • send • sleep • tell • throw

a) Fiona ______________ her homework on the bus.

b) Marie ______________ us a really funny joke.

c) I ______________ for ten hours last night!

d) They ______________ their jackets in the cupboard.

e) Luke ______________ the ball to Jack.

f) My parents ______________ to the news on the radio.

g) I didn't text her. I ______________ her an e-mail.

Hast du das Lösungswort herausgefunden?

Lösungswort: | | | | | | | |

## 5 Gemischte Formen (*Mixed forms*)

●○○ 1. Schreibe die Sätze um – in die bejahte Form, wenn er verneint ist und in die verneinte Form, wenn er bejaht ist. → Lösung S. 57

a) I saw Susie in town today.

________________________________________

b) They didn't forget my birthday.

________________________________________

c) Martin felt very hungry.

________________________________________

d) Jenny didn't lose her keys.

________________________________________

e) We understood the question.

________________________________________

●○○ 2. Ergänze den Text mit den richtigen Verbformen. → Lösung S. 57

Something exciting __________ (happen) to me last week. On Monday morning, I __________ (get) up at half past seven as usual and __________ (go) to school. But on the way I __________ (see) something on the street and I __________ (stop) to take a closer look. It __________ (be) a small bag full of money! I __________ (not/know) what to do, so I __________ (decide) to take it to the police station. The police __________ (take) the bag and __________ (write) down my name and phone number. After that, I __________ (forget) all about it. So it __________ (be) a really big surprise when the police m) __________ (phone) me on Friday! It __________ (be) an old lady's bag, and she __________ (want) to give me £ 200 because I __________ (find) her money!

●○○ 3. Verbinde die zwei Satzhälften, die zusammengehören. → Lösung S. 57

| | |
|---|---|
| a) Melanie lost | the film. |
| b) They invited us | three kilometres yesterday. |
| c) I didn't remember | her keys last week. |
| d) We really enjoyed | at 12 o'clock. |
| e) Jim ran | his name. |
| f) The children ate | because it was boring. |
| g) The lesson ended | to their Christmas party. |
| h) I didn't like this book | all the cakes. |

●○○ 4. Bejaht oder verneint? Markiere die richtige Form. → Lösung S. 58

a) Sorry, I ____________ you. Please say it again.

☐ heard ☐ didn't hear

b) Lucy walked home because she ____________ the bus.

☐ missed ☐ didn't miss

c) The teacher asked me a question but I ____________ the answer.

☐ knew ☐ didn't know

d) Angie ____________ on time. She was 30 minutes late.

☐ arrived ☐ didn't arrive

e) We ____________ a really great time! Thank you!

☐ had ☐ didn't have

f) You didn't know where to go because you ____________ to me.

☐ listened ☐ didn't listen

g) I haven't got a phone. I ____________ it last week.

☐ lost ☐ didn't lose

## 6 Fragen und Antworten (*Questions and answers*)

●○○ 1. Beantworte die Fragen mit einem ganzen Satz. → Lösung S. 58

a) Did you watch the football match last night?

No, ______________________________.

b) Did John sell his old car?

Yes, ______________________________.

c) Did Josie and Ben go shopping?

No, ______________________________.

d) Did Anna tell you the news?

Yes, ______________________________.

●○○ 2. Gegeben sind die Antworten, welche Fragen wurden gestellt? Die Bilder helfen dir. → Lösung S. 58

a) I went to the cinema last Saturday.

______________________________

b) We had breakfast at 8 o'clock.

______________________________

c) Tom bought some new jeans.

______________________________

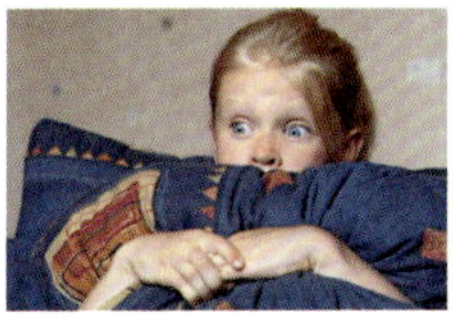

d) No, I didn't like the film.

______________________________

●●○ 3. Wo haben sich hier Fehler eingeschlichen? → Lösung S. 58

a) Did their team won the match last week?

_______________________________________________

b) No, I didn't went swimming yesterday.

_______________________________________________

c) Where met you Adam?

_______________________________________________

d) Yes, I did tasted the soup.

_______________________________________________

e) Did you your homework yesterday?

_______________________________________________

●●○ 4. Ergänze die Dialoge. → Lösung S. 58

a) A: My grandparents went on holiday last week.
B: Where _______________________________________?
A: To Spain.

b) A: I went to a great new Italian restaurant at the weekend!
B: Really? What _______________________________________?
A: A delicious cheese pizza!

c) A: Do you want to look at some photos?
B: They're great! Did _______________________________________?
A: No, I didn't. My sister took them.

d) A: I went for a long run yesterday.
B: How far _______________________________________?
A: Eight kilometres.

## 1 Aussprache und Schreibung (*Pronunciation and spelling*)

Übungen ab S. 44

1.

| [d] | [t] | [ɪd] |
|---|---|---|
| agreed | asked | corrected |
| arrived | checked | invited |
| called | cooked | needed |
| climbed | dropped | shouted |
| danced | finished | started |
| enjoyed | helped | visited |
| followed | liked | waited |
| scored | stopped | wanted |

2. a) played b) ended c) changed d) shopped e) carried f) needed g) stopped h) tried i) believed j) laughed k) stayed l) phoned

## 2 Regelmäßige Verben (*Regular verbs*)

Übungen ab S. 45

1. a) It was hot in the room, so I **opened** the window. b) My grandparents **visited** us last weekend. c) The fire **started** in the kitchen. d) We **helped** Annie get everything ready for the party. e) A little white cat **followed** us all the way home. f) At the last minute, Tony **scored** the winning goal! g) They **listened** to the beautiful music. h) Our teacher **asked** us a lot of questions. i) Tom **needed** money, so he **looked** for a job. j) The curry **tasted** really spicy!

2. a) We **waited** for Emma for a long time, but she **didn't arrive**. b) The test was very hard. I **didn't understand** most of the questions. c) These shoes were quite cheap. They **didn't cost** much. d) I really **enjoyed** the party but I **didn't like** the food. e) We **danced** all night at Charlie's party.

3. a) Sandy cooked dinner for everyone. b) The children jumped on the bed. c) Samuel didn't clean his room. d) Pete walked his dog in the park. e) They didn't laugh at my joke. f) The team trained hard for the match.

4. a) Clara **didn't play** in the match yesterday. b) The train **stopped** at the station. c) My brother **didn't help** me with my homework. d) Mum **carried** the baby upstairs.

## 3 Die einfache Vergangenheit von *to be* (*The simple past of "to be"*)

Übungen ab S. 47

1. a) Our last tennis match **was** very exciting! b) Picasso **was** a famous painter. c) Liam and Sammy **were** at the cinema last weekend. d) It **was** very hot last summer.

2. b) They **weren't** from Spain. They were from Portugal. c) You **weren't** right. You were wrong. d) Rebecca **wasn't** at the party. She was on holiday. e) The film **wasn't** at 5 p.m. It was at 6 p.m. f) We **weren't** at the train station. We were at the bus station. g) Her jacket **wasn't** red. It was black. h) Paul and Andy **weren't** at the pizzeria. They were at the café.

3. b) Was the test easy? c) Was that your sister? d) Were your parents angry with you last night? e) Was it Tim's birthday yesterday? f) Were the flowers for your mum?

4. a) Yes, **he was**. b) No, **they weren't**. c) Yes, **I was**. d) No, **it wasn't**. e) Yes, **they were**. f) No, **she wasn't**. g) Yes, **it was**. h) No, **they weren't**.

## 4 Unregelmäßige Formen (*Irregular forms*)

Übungen ab S. 49

1.

| infinitive | simple past | infinitive | simple past |
|---|---|---|---|
| (to) break | broke | (to) buy | bought |
| (to) come | came | (to) drink | drank |
| (to) eat | ate | (to) find | found |
| (to) give | gave | (to) go | went |
| (to) leave | left | (to) meet | met |
| (to) take | took | (to) write | wrote |
| (to) have | had | (to) see | saw |
| (to) get | got | (to) do | did |
| (to) stand | stood | (to) read | read |
| (to) swim | swam | (to) fall | fell |
| (to) think | thought | (to) make | made |
| (to) know | knew | (to) sell | sold |

2. a) I once **met** a very famous singer! b) She **bought** some beautiful flowers for her mother. c) Jake **gave** me his new phone number. d) The skiing trip wasn't much fun. I **broke** my leg! e) Jessie **went** to the shopping centre to buy some new shoes. f) Marc isn't here now. He **left** ten minutes ago. g) I **found** this phone in the playground. Is it yours? h) We were thirsty, so we **drank** some water.

3.

| | | | | | | | | | |
|---|---|---|---|---|---|---|---|---|---|
| a) | | | D | I | D | | | | |
| b) | | T | O | L | D | | | | |
| c) | | S | L | E | P | T | | | |
| d) | | | P | U | T | | | | |
| e) | | T | H | R | E | W | | | |
| f) | | L | I | S | T | E | N | E | D |
| g) | S | E | N | T | | | | | |

Lösungswort:

| | | | | | | |
|---|---|---|---|---|---|---|
| D | O | L | P | H | I | N |

## 5 Gemischte Formen (*Mixed forms*)

Übungen ab S. 51

1. I didn't see Susie in town today. b) They forgot my birthday. c) Martin didn't feel very hungry. d) Jenny lost her keys. e) We didn't understand the question.

2. Something exciting **happened** to me last week. On Monday morning, I **got** up at half past seven as usual, and **went** to school. But on the way I **saw** something on the street and I **stopped** take a closer look. It **was** a small bag full of money! I **didn't know** what to do, so I **decided** to take it to the police station. The police **took** the bag and **wrote** down my name and phone number. After that, I **forgot** all about it. So it **was** a really big surprise when the police **phoned** me on Friday! It **was** an old lady's bag, and she **wanted** to give me £ 200 because I **found** her money!

3. b) They invited us to their Christmas party. c) I didn't remember his name. d) We really enjoyed the film. e) Jim ran three kilometers yesterday. f) The children ate all the cakes. g) The lesson ended at 12 o'clock. h) I didn't like this book because it was boring.

4. a) Sorry, I **didn't hear** you. Please say it again. b) Lucy walked home because she **missed** the bus. c) The teacher asked me a question but I **didn't know** the answer. d) Angie **didn't arrive** on time. She was 30 minutes late. e) We **had** a really great time! Thank you! f) You don't know where to go because you **didn't listen** to me. g) I haven't got a phone. I **lost** it last week.

## 6 Fragen und Antworten (*Questions and answers*)

→ Übungen ab S. 53

1. a) No, I didn't watch the football match last night. b) Yes, he sold his old car. c) No, they didn't go shopping. d) Yes, she told me the news.

2. a) Where did you go last Saturday? b) When / What time did you have breakfast? c) What did Tom buy? d) Did you like the film?

3. a) Did their team **win** the match last week? b) No, I didn't **go** swimming yesterday. c) Where **did you meet** Adam? d) Yes, **I tasted** the soup. e) **Did you do** your homework yesterday?

4. a) Where did they go? b) What did you eat/have? c) Did you take them? d) How far did you run?

# Die Verlaufsform der Gegenwart (*The present progressive*)

## 1 Einfache Form und Verlaufsform (*Simple present and present progressive*)

●○○ 1. Verändere die Sätze so, dass etwas gerade jetzt geschieht. Dazu brauchst du das *present progressive*. → Lösung S. 61

a) I often send texts to my best friend.

Just now, I'm sending a text to my best friend.

b) David sometimes has lunch in the school cafeteria.

Today ______________________________

c) My grandmother always watches TV in the evening.

At the moment ______________________________

d) I always do my homework after school.

______________________________

●○○ 2. Setze ein: *simple present* oder *present progressive*. → Lösung S. 61

a) Look at Marie! She ____________ (take) another selfie!

b) I ____________ (not/ride) my bike in winter.

c) Paula never ____________ (listen) to rock music.

d) It's hot today so the children ____________ (play) in the garden.

e) "What ____________ (you/do)?" "We ____________ (look) at some photos."

f) Charlie often ____________ (help) his dad in the garden.

g) I ____________ (not/enjoy) this film. Let's go home!

## 2 Verlaufsform mit futurischer Bedeutung (*Present progressive with future meaning*)

●○○ 1. Was plant die Klasse für ihren London Ausflug? → Lösung S. 61

**Class 6b – Trip to London**

| | |
|---|---|
| **Monday:** | arrive in London / go to Buckingham Palace |
| **Tuesday:** | take a boat trip on the River Thames / see the Houses of Parliament and Big Ben / ride on the London Eye |
| **Wednesday:** | visit the Natural History and Science Museums |
| **Thursday:** | fly home |

a) What are the pupils in Class 6b doing on Monday?

*They are arriving in London and going to Buckingham Palace.*

b) When are they taking a boat trip?

________________________________________

c) Are they riding on the London Eye on Monday?

________________________________________

d) What are they doing on Wednesday?

________________________________________

e) Are they staying in London on Thursday?

________________________________________

●○○ 2. Bilde ganze Sätze. Benutze dabei die Verlaufsform. → Lösung S. 61

a) Lucy / have / a / party / tomorrow

________________________________________

b) We / plan / a / surprise / for / Jenny's / birthday

________________________________________

c) They / meet / us / at / 6 o'clock

________________________________________

## 1 Einfache Form und Verlaufsform (*Simple present and present progressive*)

→ Übungen ab S. 59

1. b) Today David **is having** lunch in the school cafeteria. c) At the moment my grandmother **is watching** TV. d) **I'm doing** my homework now.

2. a) Look at Marie! She **is taking** another selfie! b) I **don't ride** my bike in winter. c) Paula never **listens** to rock music. d) It's hot today so the children **are playing** in the garden. e) "What **are you doing**?" "We **are looking** at some photos." f) Charlie often **helps** his dad in the garden. g) I **am not enjoying** this film. Let's go home!

## 2 Verlaufsform mit futurischer Bedeutung (*Present progressive with future meaning*)

→ Übungen ab S. 60

1. b) They're taking a boat trip on Tuesday. c) No, they're riding on the London Eye on Tuesday. d) They're visiting the Natural History and Science Museums. e) No, they're flying home on Thursday.

2. a) Lucy's having a party tomorrow. b) We're planning a surprise for Jenny's birthday. c) They're meeting us at 6 o'clock.

# Die Verlaufsform der Vergangenheit (*The past progressive*)

## 1 Die Verlaufsform (*The past progressive*)

●○○ 1. Was ist zu einer bestimmten Zeit in der Vergangenheit geschehen? Verwende das *past progressive*.

→ Lösung S. 64

| Last Saturday | Emily | Jim and Mike |
|---|---|---|
| at 7 a.m. | sleep | have breakfast |
| at 9.30 a.m. | surf online | play tennis |
| at 1 p.m. | listen to music | swim |
| at 4.45 p.m. | text her friends | ride their bikes |

a) At 7 a.m., Emily was sleeping.

b) At 7 a.m., Jim and Mike

c) __________

d) __________

e) __________

f) __________

g) __________

h) __________

●○○ 2. Ergänze die Sätze mit der Verlaufsform der Vergangenheit.

→ Lösung S. 64

a) At 7.30 this morning I __________ (wait) for the bus.

b) Louise __________ (do) her homework in the lunch break.

c) We saw Liam and Oscar. They __________ (play) basketball.

d) Where were you this morning? We __________ (wait) for you!

## 2 Einfache Form und Verlaufsform (*Simple past and past progressive*)

●○○ 1. Was passierte, als etwas Anderes noch nicht abgeschlossen war? Schreibe im *past progressive*. → Lösung S 64

a) We ________________ lunch when the phone rang.

b) They ________________ football when it started to rain.

c) I ________________ my homework when my mum came in.

d) Emma ________________ glasses when I saw her yesterday.

●●○ 2. Ergänze mit der richtigen Vergangenheitsform. → Lösung S. 64

a) I ____________________________ (send) Eva a text when she ____________________________ (come) into the room.

b) Luke ____________________________ (lose) his keys while he ____________________________ (jog) in the park.

c) We ____________________________ (finish) the English test when the school bell ____________________________ (ring).

d) Lara ____________________________ (hurt) her foot while she ____________________________ (climb) in the mountains.

## 1 Die Verlaufsform (*The past progressive*)

→ Übungen ab S. 62

1. b) At 7 a.m., Jim and Mike **were having** breakfast. c) At 9.30 a.m., Emily **was surfing** online. d) At 9.30 a.m., Jim and Mike **were playing** tennis. e) At 1 p.m., Emily was listening to music. f) At 1 p.m., Jim and Mike **were swimming**. g) At 4.45 p.m., Emily **was texting** her friends. h) At 4.45 p.m., Jim and Mike **were riding** their bikes.

2. a) At 7.30 this morning, I **was waiting** for the bus. b) Louise **was doing** her homework in the lunch break. c) We saw Liam and Oscar. They **were playing** basketball. d) Where were you this morning? We **were waiting** for you!

## 2 Einfache Form und Verlaufsform (*Simple past and past progressive*)

→ Übungen ab S. 63

1. a) We **were having** lunch when the phone rang. b) They **were playing** football when it started to rain. c) I **was doing** my homework when my mum came in. d) Emma **was wearing** glasses when I saw her yesterday.

2. a) I **was sending** Eva a text when she **came** into the room b) Luke **lost** his keys while he **was jogging** in the park. c) We **were finishing** the English test when the school bell **rang**. d) Lara **hurt** her foot while she **was climbing** in the mountains.

# Das Futur (*Future tenses*)

## 1 Das Futur mit *going to* (*The going to future*)

1. Für Absichten und Pläne verwendest du das Futur mit *going to*. Bilde Sätze, die die Absicht ausdrücken. → Lösung S. 73

a) Tina has got some eggs, flour and sugar. (cake)

She's going to make a cake.

b) The children are wearing pyjamas and cleaning their teeth. (bed)

______________________________

c) Brian is writing something on his phone. (text)

______________________________

d) Cathy and Rob have got some sandwiches and crisps. (lunch)

______________________________

e) Harry has got some paper and colouring pencils. (picture)

______________________________

f) Maya is in a shop, holding a comic and some money. (buy)

______________________________

2. Ergänze die Sätze mit der Verneinung *not going to*. → Lösung S. 73

a) I ____________ learn any English vocabulary today.

b) Katie ____________ come with us today. She's busy.

c) You should clean your room yourself – we ____________ going to help you!

d) They ____________ invite all their friends to the party.

e) I ____________ go outside now – it's too cold!

## 2 Das Futur mit *going to* – Fragen und Kurzantworten (*The going to future – questions and short answers*)

●○○ 1. In Fragen ändert sich die Satzstellung – Schreibe Fragen und Kurzantworten mit dem *going to* Futur. → Lösung S. 73

a) Mrs Collins / give / us / a lot of homework / tomorrow? – Yes

________________________________________

b) you / bring / Jamie / to the party? – No

________________________________________

c) they / listen to / their new CD / later? – Yes

________________________________________

d) we / miss / train? – No

________________________________________

e) Tom / walk / dog / after school? – Yes

________________________________________

●○○ 2. Vervollständige die Fragen mit *going to* und einem der folgenden Verben. Schreibe die Kurzantwort dazu. → Lösung S. 73

be • like • meet • phone • post • visit

a) ________ Linda ________________ these photos on the website? –

No, ________________

b) ________ your parents ________________ the present? –

Yes, ________________

c) ________ you ________________ me at the station? –

Yes, ________________

d) ________ we ________________ the old castle? –

No, ________________

e) ________ I ________________ late? –

Yes, ________________

## 3 Das Futur mit *will* (*Will future*)

●○○ 1. Ergänze *will* und ein passendes Verb. → Lösung S. 73

answer • be • collect • eat • give • need • rain • send • take • win

a) We ______________ some money for the school trip.

b) Mrs Grant ______________ the money tomorrow.

c) Ask Mr Milton. He ______________ your questions.

d) I don't have time for lunch. I ______________ a sandwich later.

e) "Where's Chris?" "I don't know. I ______________ him a text."

f) They don't think Richard ______________ the race.

g) The weather is always bad in England! I know it ______________ while we're there!

h) I ______________ you my phone number, then you can call me.

i) "My camera is broken." "Don't worry. Tom ______________ some photos with his phone."

j) Why don't you come with us? I'm sure Claire ______________ happy to see you!

●○○ 2. Verbinde die beiden passenden Satzhälften. → Lösung S. 73

| | |
|---|---|
| a) It's very cold. I think | move those boxes. |
| b) I hope Adam | it'll snow later. |
| c) That's a great present. I'm sure | the film. |
| d) I promise I'll help you | the kitchen for you. |
| e) I don't think Germany | us a test tomorrow. |
| f) I hope you'll enjoy | will be at the party. |
| g) I'm sure Mrs Brown will give | will win the next World Cup. |
| h) I promise I'll clean | Annie will like it. |

## 4 Das Futur mit *will* – Verneinung (*Will future – negation*)

●○○ 1. Bringe die Sätze in die verneinte Form. → Lösung S. 74

a) I'll meet you at three o'clock.

I won't meet you at three o'clock.

b) They'll miss the bus.

c) Marc will get up early tomorrow.

d) I'll need a warm jacket.

e) Dad will pay for our tickets.

f) Our class will win the competition.

●○○ 2. Bilde aus den Wörtern ganze Sätze. Verwende dabei die verneinte Form des *will future*. → Lösung S. 74

a) they / not / come / at 3 o'clock / they / come / at 4 o'clock

b) it / not / rain / tomorrow / it / be / sunny

c) we / not / have / German / test / next week / we / have / English / test

d) I / not / invite / Harry / I / invite / Simon

## 5 Das Futur mit *will* – Fragen und Antworten (*Will future – questions and answers*)

●○○ 1. Beantworte die Fragen mit Kurzantworten. → Lösung S. 74

a) Will Mum drive us to the concert? – Yes, ______________________ .

b) Will it be cold tomorrow? – No, ______________________ .

c) Will you walk the dog for me today? – Yes, ______________________ .

d) Will Tim remember to phone me? – No, ______________________ .

e) Will Amelia join the computer club? – Yes, ______________________ .

f) Will Mr Simms tell us the answers? – No, ______________________ .

g) Will you and Annie be at the party? – Yes, ______________________ .

h) Will they finish all the exercises today? – No, ______________________ .

●○○ 2. Stelle Fragen und beantworte sie. Die Tabelle hilft dir. → Lösung S. 74

| Who | Where | When |
|---|---|---|
| Catherine | school | 9.30 a.m. |
| David | swimming pool | 4 p.m. |
| Olivia | guitar lesson | 5.15 p.m. |
| Ian | cinema | 6.30 p.m. |
| Gracie | friend's house | 7.45 p.m. |
| Dylan | home | 9 p.m. |

a) *Where will Catherine be at 9.30 a.m.? – She'll be at school.*

b) ______________________

c) ______________________

d) ______________________

e) ______________________

f) ______________________

●○○ 3. Ergänze die Fragen mit *will* und einem passenden Verb. → Lösung S. 74

arrive • bark • be • do • eat • have • invite • sing

a) Who ______________ they ______________ to their party?

b) What time ______________ everyone ______________ ?

c) I'm cooking curry tonight. ______________ you ______________ it?

d) When ______________ Patrick ______________ his homework?

e) ______________ we ______________ time to visit Auntie Tessa tomorrow?

f) When ______________ you ______________ ready?

g) You have a beautiful voice. ______________ you ______________ for us later?

h) ______________ your dog ______________ when he sees me?

●●○ 4. Welche Frage passt zu den gegebenen Antworten? → Lösung S. 74

a) I'll be 14 on my next birthday.

*How old will you be on your next birthday?*

b) Yes, I'll give Frank your message.

______________________________

c) We'll be at school at 9 o'clock tomorrow morning.

Where ______________________________

d) The match will finish at half past five.

What time ______________________________

e) No, Christina won't enjoy that film.

______________________________

f) I'll send about 20 texts today!

How many ______________________________

## 6 Gemischte Formen – *going to* oder *will* (*Mixed forms – going to or will*)

●○○ 1. Benutze richtig: *will* oder *going to*. → Lösung S. 75

a) It __________________ snow later today. I heard it on the radio.

b) I don't think it __________________ snow today. It isn't cold enough.

c) Be quiet! You __________________ wake the baby!

d) Mum __________________ be angry when she sees the mess in the kitchen!

e) I think people __________________ fly to Australia in four hours in the year 2075.

f) John hopes he __________________ have time to visit us in summer.

g) I __________________ get my hair cut this afternoon.

h) Jackie __________________ meet us at 5 o'clock.

i) It's very hot in here. I __________________ open the window.

j) Eva is putting her cycling helmet on. She __________________ ride her bike.

k) We __________________ watch a film in our German lesson tomorrow.

●○○ 2. Füge die Verneinung von *will* oder *going to* ein. → Lösung S. 75

a) Philip isn't good at maths. I'm sure he __________________ pass the test.

b) No, we __________________ walk home. It's too far.

c) Ben doesn't really like Lara. He __________________ ask her out.

d) Thomas __________________ eat this. He's allergic to strawberries.

e) I __________________ go with you to the cinema today. I've already seen that film.

●○○ 3. Was gehört in die Lücke?
Kreuze die richtige Verbform an.

→ Lösung S. 75

a) Goodbye, Gracie! I ______ you!

☐ will never forget ☐ am never going to forget

b) ______ this film or can I watch the music show?

☐ Will you watch ☐ Are you going to watch

c) "I can't understand this German website." "Don't worry. I ______ for you."

☐ will translate ☐ am going to translate

d) Look at Zoe's pink hair! I don't think her mum ______ it!

☐ will like ☐ is going to like

e) "I've lost my phone!" "Oh no! I hope you ______ it soon."

☐ will find ☐ you're going to find

f) We're putting on our sports clothes because we ______ running.

☐ will go ☐ are going to go

g) If you wait a minute, Helen ______ to the station in her car.

☐ will take ☐ is going to take

●○○ 4. Schreibe Sätze mit dem Verb in Klammern
und verwende *will* oder *going to*.

→ Lösung S. 75

a) I'm really tired. I think ____________________ (go) to bed now.

b) My parents ____________________ (buy) a new car at the weekend.

c) We ____________________ (celebrate) my brother's birthday at our favourite Chinese restaurant.

d) Who ____________________ (be) the next President of the United States?

e) In ten years, nearly everyone ____________________ (have) a mobile phone.

## 1 Das Futur mit *going to* (*The going to future*)

Übungen ab S. 65

1. b) They are going to go to bed. c) He's going to send a text. d) They're going to have lunch. e) He's going to draw a picture. f) She's going to buy a comic.

2. a) I **am not going to** learn any English vocabulary today. b) Katie **isn't going to** come with us today. She's busy. c) You should clean your room yourself – we **aren't going to** help you! d) They **aren't going to** invite all their friends to the party. e) I**'m not going to** go outside now – it's too cold!

## 2 Das Futur mit *going to* – Fragen und Kurzantworten (*The going to future – questions and short answers*)

Übungen ab S. 66

1. Is Mrs Collins going to give us a lot of homework tomorrow? – Yes, she is. b) Are you going to bring Jamie to the party? – No, I'm not. c) Are they going to listen to their new CD later? – Yes, they are. d) Are we going to miss the train? – No, we/you aren't. e) Is Tom going to walk the dog after school? – Yes, he is.

2. a) **Is** Linda **going to post** these photos on the website? – No, **she isn't**. b) **Are** your parents **going to like** the present? – Yes, **they are**. c) **Are** you **going to meet** me at the station? – Yes, **I am**. d) **Are** we **going to visit** the old castle? – No, **we/you aren't**. e) **Am I going to be** late? – Yes, **you are**.

## 3 Das Futur mit *will* (*Will future*)

Übungen ab S. 67

1. a) We **will need** some money for the school trip. b) Mrs Grant **will collect** the money tomorrow. c) Ask Mr Milton. He **will answer** your questions. d) I don't have time for lunch. I **will eat** a sandwich later. e) "Where's Chris?" "I don't know. I **will send** him a text." f) They don't think Richard **will win** the race. g) The weather is always bad in England. I know it **will rain** while we're there! h) I **will give** you my phone number, then you can call me. i) "My camera is broken." "Don't worry. Tom **will take** some photos with his phone. j) Why don't you come with us? I'm sure Claire **will be** happy to see you!

2. b) I hope Adam will be at the party. c) That's a great present. I'm sure Annie will like it. d) I promise I'll help you move those boxes. e) I don't think Germany will win the next World Cup. f) I hope you'll enjoy the film. g) I'm sure Mrs Brown will give us a test tomorrow. h) I promise I'll clean the kitchen for you.

## 4 Das Futur mit *will* – Verneinung (*Will future – negation*)

Übungen ab S. 68

1. b) They won't miss the bus. c) Marc won't get up early tomorrow. d) I won't need a warm jacket. e) Dad won't pay for our tickets. f) Our class won't win the competition.

2. a) They won't come at 3 o'clock. They'll come at 4 o'clock. b) It won't rain tomorrow. It'll be sunny. c) We won't have a German test next week. We'll have an English test. d) I won't invite Harry. I'll invite Simon.

## 5 Das Futur mit *will* – Fragen und Antworten (*Will future – questions and answers*)

Übungen ab S. 69

1. a) Yes, **she will**. b) No, **it won't**. c) Yes, **I will**. d) No, **he won't**. e) Yes, **she will**. f) No, **he won't**. g) Yes, **we will**. h) No, **they won't**.

2. b) Where will David be at 4 p.m.? – He'll be at the swimming pool. c) Where will Olivia be at 5.15 p.m.? – She'll be at her guitar lesson. d) Where will Ian be at 6.30 p.m.? – He'll be at the cinema. e) Where will Gracie be at 7.45 p.m.? – She'll be at her friend's house. f) Where will Dylan be at 9 p.m.? – He'll be at home.

3. a) Who **will** they **invite** to their party? b) What time **will** everyone **arrive**? c) I'm cooking curry tonight. **Will** you **eat** it? d) When **will** Patrick **do** his homework? e) **Will** we **have** time to visit Auntie Tessa tomorrow? f) When **will** you **be** ready? g) You have a beautiful voice. **Will** you **sing** for us later? h) **Will** your dog **bark** when he sees me?

4. b) Will you give Frank my message? c) Where will you be at 9 o'clock tomorrow morning? d) What time will the match finish? e) Will Christina enjoy that film? f) How many texts will you send today?

## 6 Gemischte Formen – *going to* oder *will* (*Mixed forms – going to or will*)

Übungen ab S. 71

1. a) It**'s going to** snow later. I heard it on the radio this morning. b) I don't think it **will** snow today. It isn't cold enough. c) Be quiet! You **will** wake the baby! d) Mum **will** be angry when she sees the mess in the kitchen. e) I think people **will** fly to Australia in four hours in the year 2075. f) John hopes he **will** have time to visit us in summer. g) I **am going to** get my hair cut this afternoon. h) Jackie **is going to** meet us at 5 o'clock. i) It's very hot in here. I **will** open the window. j) Eva is putting her cycling helmet on. She **is going to** ride her bike. k) We **are going to** watch a film in our German lesson tomorrow.

2. a) Philip isn't good at maths. I'm sure he **won't** pass the test. b) No, we **are not going to** walk home. It's too far. c) Ben doesn't really like Lara. He **isn't going to** ask her out. d) Thomas **won't** eat this. He's allergic to strawberries. e) I **am not going to go** with you to the cinema today. I've already seen that film.

3. a) Goodbye, Gracie! I **will never forget** you! b) **Are you going to watch** this film or can I watch the music show? c) "I can't understand this German website." "Don't worry. I **will translate** it for you. d) Look at Zoe's pink hair! I don't think her mum **will like** it! e) "I've lost my phone!" "Oh no! I hope you **will find** it soon." f) We're putting on our sports clothes because we **are going to go** running. g) If you wait a minute, Helen **will take** you to the station in her car.

4. a) I'm really tired. I think I **will go** to bed now. b) My parents **are going to buy** a new car at the weekend. c) We **are going to celebrate** my brother's birthday at our favourite Chinese restaurant. d) Who **will be** the next President of the United States? e) In ten years, everyone **will have** a mobile phone.

# Das Perfekt (*The present perfect*)

## 1 Das Partizip Perfekt (*The past participle*)

●○○ 1. Ergänze in der Tabelle die Verbformen von *simple past* und *present perfect*. (= Partizip Perfekt/*past participle*) → Lösung S. 83

| | infinitive | simple past | past participle |
|---|---|---|---|
| a) | (to) answer | | |
| b) | (to) buy | | |
| c) | (to) come | | |
| d) | (to) do | | |
| e) | (to) find | | |
| f) | (to) get | | |
| g) | (to) have | | |
| h) | (to) kick | | |
| i) | (to) leave | | |
| j) | (to) meet | | |
| k) | (to) put | | |
| l) | (to) smile | | |

●○○ 2. Wie lautet das Partizip Perfekt richtig? → Lösung S. 83

a) (to) give: ☐ gived ☐ given ☐ gave
b) (to) drive: ☐ driven ☐ droven ☐ drove
c) (to) eat: ☐ ate ☐ eated ☐ eaten
d) (to) write: ☐ written ☐ wroten ☐ wrote
e) (to) swim: ☐ swam ☐ swum ☐ swom
f) (to) see: ☐ sawn ☐ seen ☐ saw
g) (to) drink: ☐ drunk ☐ drank ☐ drunken
h) (to) go: ☐ went ☐ goed ☐ gone

## 2 Bejahte Aussagesätze (*Positive statements*)

●○○ 1. Verbinde die Sätze, die zusammenpassen. → Lösung S. 83

| | |
|---|---|
| a) Max isn't here. | I've lost my mobile. |
| b) I've got a lot of homework. | We've missed it! |
| c) We're not hungry now. | They've won all their matches this year. |
| d) Marie is very rich. | He's gone home. |
| e) I can't phone anyone. | The leaves have fallen off the trees. |
| f) Oh no! There goes the bus! | She's just bought a Porsche. |
| g) That team is very good. | I haven't finished it yet. |
| h) It's winter now. | We've just had lunch. |

●○○ 2. Ergänze die Sätze mit einem Verb im *present perfect*. → Lösung S. 83

break • drink • enjoy • finish • forget • make • paint • tell • watch

a) Look – Claire ____________ her keys!

b) You ____________ enough TV today. Go and play outside now.

c) Someone ____________ all the lemonade. The bottle is empty!

d) The children ____________ some pictures for the classroom wall.

e) Paul ____________ some cookies. Would you like one?

f) "Why are you laughing?" "Jake ____________ just ____________ us a great joke!"

g) Put your plates in the dishwasher when you ____________ your breakfast.

h) Thank you for a lovely day! We ____________ it!

i) Ben can't walk because he ____________ his leg.

3. Was ist gerade passiert? Schreibe Sätze mit *just*. → Lösung S. 83

a) She ________ (wake up)

b) He ________ (score)

c) She ________ (send)

d) They ________ (buy)

e) The train ________ (arrive)

f) The lesson ________ (start)

4. Bilde aus den Sätzen einen Satz im *present perfect*. → Lösung S. 83

a) Jim can't find his jacket. (lose)

He's lost his jacket.

b) Carrie is lying on the floor. (fall over)

________________________________

c) Mrs Jackson isn't in the room now. (leave)

________________________________

d) It was snowing this morning, but now it isn't snowing. (stop)

________________________________

## 3 Verneinte Aussagesätze (*Negative statements*)

●○○ 1. Verneine die folgenden Sätze. → Lösung S. 84

a) I've been to New York.

I haven't been to New York.

b) We've known Lily for a long time.

c) Chris has walked the dog today.

d) They've had their breakfast.

e) Sam has done his homework.

●○○ 2. Schreibe aus den Stichwörtern Sätze im *present perfect*. → Lösung S. 84

a) I / not / speak / to / Daniel / yet

b) Liam / not / start / book / report

c) they / not / pack / bags

d) we / not / practise / for / concert

e) Lisa / not / buy / enough / drinks / for / party

## 4 Fragen und Antworten (*Questions and answers*)

●○○ 1. Beantworte die Fragen mit Kurzantworten. → Lösung S. 84

a) Have you seen the new "X-Men" film? – Yes, ________________ .

b) Has Matthew uploaded the photos yet? – No, ________________ .

c) Has the last bus left? – Yes, ________________ .

d) Have they had a test this week? – No, ________________ .

e) Has Emma phoned you yet? – Yes, ________________ .

f) Have you sent Grandma a birthday card? – No, ________________ .

g) Has Tony bought the concert tickets? – Yes, ________________ .

h) Have they read your blog? – No, ________________ .

●●○ 2. Bilde Fragesätze. Benutze dazu ein passendes Fragewort und verwende das *present perfect*. → Lösung S. 84

how long • how many • where • which • who

a) eat / all / crisps?

________________________________________

b) you / be?

________________________________________

c) English words / you / learn / this week?

________________________________________

d) you / live / here?

________________________________________

e) texts / you / send / today?

________________________________________

## 5 Signalwörter für das Perfekt (*Signal words*)

●○○ 1. Am Signalwort erkennst du, dass das *present perfect* die richtige Zeitform ist. Welches Signalwort passt? → Lösung S. 84

a) Have you ________________ been to Norway?

☐ already ☐ ever ☐ yet

b) I ordered a book but it hasn't arrived ________________ .

☐ yet ☐ just ☐ never

c) No, David isn't here now. He's ________________ left.

☐ ever ☐ so far ☐ just

d) Wow! They've ________________ won four matches this month!

☐ already ☐ never ☐ yet

e) How many glasses of cola have you drunk ________________ today?

☐ just ☐ so far ☐ ever

f) No, I've ________________ met a famous film star.

☐ ever ☐ yet ☐ never

●○○ 2. Beantworte die Fragen, verwende *yet* oder *already*. → Lösung S. 84

a) Have you done your maths homework yet? (Yes)

*Yes, I've already done it.*

b) Has the film started yet? (No)

________________________________________

c) Has James written the e-mail yet? (Yes)

________________________________________

d) Have the children cleaned their room yet? (No)

________________________________________

●●○ 3. Bilde ganze Sätze im *Present Perfect* und ergänze *since* oder *for*.

→ Lösung S. 84

| | Who | What | Time |
|---|---|---|---|
| a) | Charlotte | know Chris | six months |
| b) | I | not phoned my aunt | Christmas |
| c) | They | live in that house | ages |
| d) | Peter | not be to the cinema | more than two weeks |
| e) | Joanna | not ill | 2012 |
| f) | We | be here | 5 o'clock |
| g) | Julia | has this computer | one year |
| h) | I | not see Frank | last June |

a) *Charlotte has known Chris for six months.*

b) ____________________

c) ____________________

d) ____________________

e) ____________________

f) ____________________

g) ____________________

h) ____________________

●●○ 4. Füge das Signalwort an der richtigen Stelle ein.

→ Lösung S. 84

a) Tim ______ has ______ got ______ up ______ . (just)

b) I ______ have ______ been ______ to Scotland ______ . (never)

c) They ______ have ______ answered ______ all the questions. (so far)

d) We ______ haven't ______ listened ______ to the song ______ . (yet)

e) Has ______ Karen ______ met ______ your brother ______ ? (ever)

## 1 Das Partizip Perfekt (*The past participle*)

Übungen ab S. 76

1.

| | infinitive | simple past | past participle |
|---|---|---|---|
| a) | (to) answer | answered | answered |
| b) | (to) buy | bought | bought |
| c) | (to) come | came | come |
| d) | (to) do | did | done |
| e) | (to) find | found | found |
| f) | (to) get | got | got |
| g) | (to) have | had | had |
| h) | (to) kick | kicked | kicked |
| i) | (to) leave | left | left |
| j) | (to) meet | met | met |
| k) | (to) put | put | put |
| l) | (to) smile | smiled | smiled |

2. a) given b) driven c) eaten d) written e) swum f) seen g) drunk h) gone

## 2 Bejahte Aussagesätze (*Positive statements*)

Übungen ab S. 77

1. a) Max isn't here. He's gone home. b) I've got a lot of homework today. I haven't finished it yet. c) We're not hungry now. We've just had lunch. d) Marie is very rich. She's just bought a Porsche. e) I can't phone anyone. I've lost my mobile. f) Oh no! There goes the bus! We've missed it! g) That team is very good. They've won all their matches this year. h) It's winter now. The leaves have fallen off the trees.

2. a) Look – Claire **has forgotten** her keys. b) You **have watched** enough TV today. Go and play outside now. c) Someone **has drunk** all the lemonade. The bottle is empty! d) The children **have painted** some pictures for the classroom wall. e) Paul **has made** some cookies. Would you like one? f) "Why are you laughing?" "Jake **has** just **told** us a great joke!" g) Put your plates in the dishwasher when you **have finished** your breakfast h) Thank you for a lovely day! We **have enjoyed** it! i) Ben can't walk because he **has broken** his leg.

3. a) She has just woken up. b) He has just scored a goal. c) She has just sent a text. d) They have just bought some ice-cream. e) The train has just arrived. f) The lesson has just started.

4. b) She's fallen over. c) She's left the room. d) It's stopped snowing.

## 3 Verneinte Aussagesätze (*Negative statements*)

Übungen ab S. 79

1. b) We haven't known Lily for a long time. c) Chris hasn't walked the dog today. d) They haven't had their breakfast. e) Sam hasn't done his homework.

2. a) I haven't spoken to Daniel yet. b) Liam hasn't started his book report. c) They haven't packed their bags. d) We haven't practised for the concert. e) Lisa hasn't bought enough drinks for the party.

## 4 Fragen und Antworten (*Questions and answers*)

Übungen ab S. 80

1. a) Yes, **I have**. b) No, **he hasn't**. c) Yes, **it has**. d) No, **they haven't**. e) Yes, **she has**. f) No, **I haven't**. g) Yes, **he has**. h) No, **they haven't**.

2. a) Who has eaten all the crisps? b) Where have you been? c) Which English words have you learned this week? d) How long have you lived here? e) How many texts have you sent today?

## 5 Signalwörter für das Perfekt (*Signal words*)

Übungen ab S. 81

1. a) Have you **ever** been to Norway? b) I ordered a book but it hasn't arrived **yet**. c) No, David isn't here now. He's **just** left. d) Wow! They've **already** won four matches this month! e) How many glasses of cola have you drunk **so far** today? f) No, I've **never** met a famous film star.

2. b) No, it hasn't started yet. c) Yes, he's already written the e-mail. d) No, they haven't cleaned their room yet.

3. b) I haven't phoned my aunt **since** Christmas. c) They have lived in that house **for** ages. d) Peter hasn't been to the cinema **for** more than two weeks. e) Joanna hasn't been ill **since** 2012. f) We've been here **since** 5 o'clock. g) Julia has had this computer **for** one year. h) I haven't seen Frank **since** last June.

4. a) Tim has **just** got up. b) I have **never** been to Scotland. c) **So far** they have answered all the questions / They have answered all the questions **so far**. d) We haven't listened to the song **yet**. e) Has Karen **ever** met your brother?

# Fragen (*Questions*)

## 1 Fragewörter (*Question words*)

●○○ 1. Markiere das richtige Fragewort. → Lösung S. 88

a) ________ film do you want to see – "James Bond" or "Star Wars"?

☐ who ☐ what ☐ which

b) ________ time do we need to leave?

☐ what ☐ how ☐ when

c) ________ are you angry with me?

☐ why ☐ what ☐ who

d) ________ has Mike invited to his birthday party?

☐ who ☐ when ☐ how

e) ________ much are the concert tickets?

☐ how ☐ who ☐ where

●●○ 2. Wie lautete die Frage zu diesen Antworten?
Frage nach den fett gedruckten Wörtern. → Lösung S. 88

a) I phoned **Gina** last night.

________________________________________

b) I drink **tea** for breakfast.

________________________________________

c) I live **near the old castle**.

________________________________________

d) Marc didn't play football yesterday **because he was ill**.

________________________________________

## 2 Fragewörter und Präpositionen (*Question words and prepositions*)

●○○ 1. Füge das richtige Verb mit Präposition in den Fragen ein.

→ Lösung S. 88

come from • get from • look at • look like • talk about • wait for

a) What does your brother ______________ ?

b) Where does Daniel ______________ ? York or Manchester?

c) I really like your shoes! Where did you __________ them __________ ?

d) Who are we ______________ ? We need to go now!

e) What did you ______________ in your tutor group yesterday?

f) "What are you ______________ ?" – "Photos of Max's holiday."

●●○ 2. Schreibe passende Fragen.

→ Lösung S. 88

a) I got my new jeans from the shopping centre. (where … from?)

*Where did you get your new jeans from?*

b) We're learning about ears and eyes in biology. (what … about?)

______________________________

c) I went to the cinema with Mike. (who … with?)

______________________________

d) Jim is looking for his keys. (what … for?)

______________________________

e) I talked to my teacher about the English test. (who … to?)

f) We wrote about our last holiday. (what … about?)

______________________________

## 3 Bestätigungsfragen (*Question tags*)

●○○ 1. Ergänze die richtige Bestätigungsfrage. → Lösung S. 88

a) It's really hot today, ____________________ ?

b) Bill can't play the guitar, ____________________ ?

c) You live in Morgan Road, ____________________ ?

d) Theresa wasn't at school yesterday, ____________________ ?

e) Marie's got a brown dog, ____________________ ?

f) Adam didn't enjoy the concert, ____________________ ?

g) You go to my school, ____________________ ?

h) Anna doesn't eat meat, ____________________ ?

i) They can ski really well, ____________________ ?

j) Peter isn't coming to the cinema with us, ____________________ ?

●○○ 2. Welches *question tag* gehört hinter den Satz – verbinde die beiden richtigen Satzteile. → Lösung S. 88

| | |
|---|---|
| a) Angela hasn't got a brother, | did he? |
| b) Your dad drives a red car, | don't you? |
| c) You can't speak Spanish, | are they? |
| d) He didn't help you with your homework | weren't they? |
| e) They aren't from London, | has she? |
| f) We've got enough time, | didn't she? |
| g) You like sushi, | can you? |
| h) Susie won the competition, | doesn't he? |
| i) The children were very hungry, | do you? |
| j) You don't go to school by bike, | haven't we? |

## 1 Fragewörter (*Question words*)

Übungen ab S. 85

1. a) **Which** film do you want to see – "James Bond" or "Star Wars"? b) **What** time do we need to leave? c) **Why** are you angry with me? d) **Who** has Mike invited to his party? e) **How much** are the concert tickets?

2. a) Who did you phone last night? b) What do you drink for breakfast? c) Where do you live? d) Why didn't Marc play football yesterday?

## 2 Fragewörter und Präpositionen (*Question words and prepositions*)

Übungen ab S. 86

1. a) What does your brother look **like**? b) Where does Daniel **come from**? York or Manchester? c) I really like your shoes! Where did you **get** them **from**? d) Who are we **waiting for**? We need to go now! e) What did you **talk about** in your tutor group yesterday? f) "What are you **looking at**?" "Photos of Max's holiday."

2. b) What are you learning about in biology? c) Who did you go to the cinema with? d) What is Jim looking for? e) Who did you talk to about the English test? f) What did you write about?

## 3 Bestätigungsfragen (*Question tags*)

Übungen ab S. 87

1. a) It's really hot today, **isn't it**? b) Bill can't play the guitar, **can he**? c) You live in Morgan Road, **don't you**? d) Theresa wasn't at school yesterday, **was she**? e) Marie's got a brown dog, **hasn't she**? f) Adam didn't enjoy the concert, **did he**? g) You go to my school, **don't you**? h) Anna doesn't eat meat, **does she**? i) They can ski really well, **can't they**? j) Peter isn't coming to the cinema with us, **is he**?

2. a) Angela hasn't got a brother, has she? b) Your dad drives a red car, doesn't he? c) You can't speak Spanish, can you? d) He didn't help you with your homework, did he? e) They aren't from London, are they? f) We've got enough time, haven't we? g) You like sushi, don't you? h) Susie won the competition, didn't she? i) The children were very hungry, weren't they? j) You don't go to school by bike, do you?

# *Present perfect* oder *simple past*?

## 1 Signalwörter (*Signal words*)

●○○ 1. Schreibe die Signalwörter in die richtige Spalte. → Lösung S.92

ago • already • ever • in 2013 • just • last month •
last Wednesday • so far • yesterday • yet

| simple past | present perfect |
|---|---|
| | |
| | |
| | |
| | |
| | |

●○○ 2. Bilde ganze Sätze im *simple past*. Stelle das Signalwort an die richtige Stelle im Satz. → Lösung S. 92

a) met / Trevor / I / ago / years / two

______________________________

b) broke / last / Tom / his / year / arm

______________________________

c) school / Caroline / in / finished / 2014

______________________________

d) have / last / we / English / didn't / lesson / Monday / an

______________________________

e) yesterday / woke / late / up / I

______________________________

## 2 *Present perfect* oder *simple past*?

●○○ 1. *Present perfect*: die Handlung hat irgendwann begonnen, ist noch nicht abgeschlossen oder dauert noch an.
*Simple past*: die Handlung ist beendet.
Was ist hier richtig?

→ ? Lösung S.92

a) Where ____________ on holiday last summer?
☐ did you go ☐ have you been

b) We ____________ school early yesterday.
☐ finished ☐ have finished

c) No, I'm not thirsty. I ____________ a bottle of water.
☐ just drank ☐ have just drunk

d) You ____________ to the teacher in that English lesson.
☐ didn't listen ☐ haven't listened

e) Oh, look! I ____________ someone's phone here on the table!
☐ found ☐ have found

●●○ 2. Bilde Fragen und Antworten.
Verwende die richtige Zeit.

→ Lösung S. 92

a) Luke / ever / be / London (yes / go / last summer)

______________________________________________

b) when / buy / your / new / skateboard (last year)

______________________________________________

c) Caroline / phone / her mother / yet (yes / this morning)

______________________________________________

d) how / much / do / homework / so far (not any yet)

______________________________________________

●●○ 3. Füge das Verb in der richtigen Form ein. → Lösung S. 92

a) It ________________ every day last week. (rain)

b) It ________________ every day this week. (rain)

c) Trisha feels sick. She ________________ too much chocolate! (eat)

d) I ________________ a really spicy curry on my last holiday. (eat)

e) Tim ________________ a new blog post. I'm going to read it later. (write)

f) Shakespeare ________________ some very famous plays. (write)

g) My brother and I once ________________ our bedroom window playing football. (break)

h) Someone ________________ this laptop! It doesn't work now. (break)

i) My grandpa died last year. He ________________ a long, interesting life. (have)

j) My granny often tells us stories. She ________________ a very interesting life. (have)

●●○ 4. Diese Sätze enthalten Fehler – findest du alle? → Lösung S. 92

a) My parents have bought this house in 2010.

________________________________________________

b) I'm waiting for a message from Ben but he didn't send it yet.

________________________________________________

c) They just opened a new shopping centre on Kings Street.

________________________________________________

d) It has snowed all day yesterday.

________________________________________________

e) Anne has arrived at half past nine this morning.

________________________________________________

## 1 Signalwörter (*Signal words*)

→ Übungen ab S. 89

1.

| simple past | present perfect |
|---|---|
| ago | already |
| in 2013 | ever |
| last month | just |
| last Wednesday | so far |
| yesterday | yet |

2. a) I met Trevor two years ago. b) Tom broke his arm last year. c) Caroline finished school in 2014. d) We didn't have an English lesson last Monday. e) I woke up late yesterday.

## 2 *Present perfect* oder *simple past*?

→ Übungen ab S. 90

1. a) Where **did you go** on holiday last year? b) We **finished** school early yesterday. c) No, I'm not thirsty. I **have just drunk** a bottle of water. d) You **didn't listen** to the teacher in that English lesson. e) Oh, look! I **have found** someone's phone here on the table!

2. a) Has Luke ever been to London? Yes, he went to London last summer. b) When did you buy your new skateboard? I bought it last year. c) Has Caroline phoned her mother yet? Yes, she phoned her this morning. d) How much homework have you done so far? I haven't done any homework yet.

3. a) It **rained** every day last week. b) It **has rained** every day this week. c) Trisha feels sick. She **has eaten** too much chocolate! d) I **ate** a really spicy curry on my last holiday. e) Tim **has written** a new blog post. I'm going to read it later. f) Shakespeare **wrote** some very famous plays. g) My brother and I once **broke** our bedroom window playing football. h) Someone **has broken** this laptop! It's doesn't work now. i) My grandpa died last year. He **had** a long, interesting life. j) My granny often tells us stories. She **has had** a very interesting life.

4. a) My parents **bought** this house in 2010. b) I'm waiting for a message from Ben but he **hasn't sent** it yet. c) They**'ve** just **opened** a new shopping centre on Kings Street. d) It **snowed** all day yesterday. e) Anne **arrived** at half past nine this morning.

# Frage nach Subjekt und Objekt (*Subject and object questions*)

## 1 Subjektfragen (*Subject questions*)

●○○ 1. Ergänze die Frage nach dem Subjekt des Satzes.
Dazu brauchst du die Fragewörter *who* oder *what*. → Lösung S. 96

a) Sam won the race. __________ was second in the race?

b) Everybody danced at the party. __________ else happened there?

c) Lily sits next to me in my classroom. __________ sits next to you?

d) I can't find my phone. __________ has seen it?

e) I like to listen to the radio in the evening. __________ helps you relax?

f) Somebody was in the kitchen. __________ broke this glass?

g) __________ takes longer – going to school by bike or by bus?

●●○ 2. Gegeben ist immer die Antwort.
Welche Frage wurde gestellt? → Lösung S. 96

a) My sister helped me with my homework.
*Who helped you with your homework?*

b) When my favourite team wins a match – that makes me happy!

__________

c) The Campbell family live next door to us.

__________

d) Flowers smell better than dirty socks!

__________

## 2 Objektfragen (*Object questions*)

●○○ 1. Für Fragen nach dem Objekt des Satzes benötigst du zusätzlich zu *who* und *what* noch das Verb (*to*) *do*. Füge das Verb für die Objektfragen ein.

→ Lösung S. 96

a) What ____________ Mrs Jones ask you in the geography lesson?

b) What ____________ they ____________ today?

c) Who ____________ your mum talk to yesterday?

d) Who ____________ you like best?

e) What ____________ you do when everybody else danced?

f) Who ____________ Gracie wait for at the station?

g) Who ____________ Lucy love?

●●○ 2. Bringe die Objektfragen in die richtige Reihenfolge.

→ Lösung S. 96

a) your / what / best / does / like / friend

______________________________________________

b) did / yesterday / say / what / Helen

______________________________________________

c) you / lunch / did / what / have / for

______________________________________________

d) she / started / the lesson / who / before / did / talk to

______________________________________________

e) cinema / at / they / what / the / watch / did

______________________________________________

f) sister / who / your / does / love

______________________________________________

## 3 Gemischte Formen (*Mixed forms*)

●○○ 1. Markiere die richtige Frage. → Lösung S. 96

a) The whole class heard a loud noise.

☐ Who heard a loud noise? ☐ Who did hear a loud noise?

b) My grandma sent me some money for my birthday.

☐ What did your grandma send you? ☐ What sent your grandma?

c) Melanie wants to come to the cinema with us.

☐ What does Melanie want? ☐ What wants Melanie?

d) Jimmy loves dogs.

☐ Who does love dogs? ☐ Who loves dogs?

●●○ 2. Nenne jeweils beide möglichen Fragen zur Antwort. → Lösung S. 96

a) Paul met Christopher.

*Who met Christopher?* / *Who did Paul meet?*

b) I lost my phone but Tim found it.

__________ / __________

c) Emma goes to Kings Road School.

__________ / __________

d) Christina waited for Jim.

__________ / __________

e) The team from England won the cup.

__________ / __________

f) Jeff Kinney wrote “Diary of a Wimpy Kid.”

__________ / __________

## 1 Subjektfragen (*Subject questions*)

Übungen ab S. 93

1. a) Sam won the race. **Who** was second in the race? b) Everybody danced at the party. **What** else happened there? c) Lily sits next to me in my classroom. **Who** sits next to you? d) I can't find my phone. **Who** has seen it? e) I like to listen to the radio in the evening. **What** helps you relax? f) Somebody was in the kitchen. **Who** broke this glass? g) **What** takes longer – going to school by bike or by bus?

2. b) What makes you happy? c) Who lives next door to you? d) Which smells better – flowers or dirty socks?

## 2 Objektfragen (*Object questions*)

Übungen ab S. 94

1. a) What **did** Mrs Jones ask you in the geography lesson? b) What **are** they **doing** today? c) Who **did** your mum talk to yesterday? d) Who **do** you like best? e) What **did** you do when everybody else danced? f) Who **does** Gracie wait for at the station? g) Who **does** Lucy love?

2. a) What does your friend like best? b) What did Helen say yesterday? c) What did you have for lunch? d) Who did she talk to before the lesson started? e) What did they watch at the cinema? f) Who does your sister love?

## 3 Gemischte Formen (*Mixed forms*)

Übungen ab S. 95

1. a) Who heard a loud noise? b) What did your grandma send you? c) What does Melanie want? d) Who loves dogs?

2. b) What did you lose? / Who found your phone? c) What school does Emma go to? / Who goes to Kings Road School? d) Who did Christina wait for? / Who waited for Jim? e) What did the team from England win? / Who won the cup? f) What did Jeff Kinney write? / Who wrote "Diary of a Wimpy Kid"?

# Die Steigerung von Adjektiven (*The comparison of adjectives*)

## 1 Steigerung mit *-er / -est* (*Comparison with -er / -est*)

●○○ 1. Einsilbige und zweisilbige Adjektive, die auf *-y* enden, werden mit *-er / -est* gesteigert.

→ Lösung S. 103

| | Grundform | 1. Steigerung | 2. Steigerung |
|---|---|---|---|
| a) | big | bigger | the biggest |
| b) | fast | | the |
| c) | cold | | the |
| d) | happy | | the |
| e) | easy | | the |

●○○ 2. Auch zweisilbige Adjektive, die auf *-le*, *-ow* oder *-er* enden, werden mit *-er / -est* gesteigert.

→ Lösung S. 103

| | Grundform | 1. Steigerung | 2. Steigerung |
|---|---|---|---|
| a) | clever | | the |
| b) | narrow | | the |
| c) | simple | | the |

●○○ 3. Füge das richtige Adjektiv mit der richtigen Steigerung ein. Du brauchst die Endungen *-er* oder *-est*.

→ Lösung S. 103

funny • long • old • quiet • young

a) The River Isar is ____________ but the River Amazon is ____________ .

b) Tom is the ____________ boy in our class.

c) Jenny tells great jokes – she's much ____________ than you!

d) I often work in the library. It's the ____________ place in the school.

## 2 Steigerung mit *more / most* (*Comparison with more / most*)

●○○ 1. Andere Adjektive werden mit *more / most* gesteigert. → Lösung S. 103

| | Grundform | 1. Steigerung | 2. Steigerung |
|---|---|---|---|
| a) | boring | more boring | the most boring |
| b) | exciting | | the |
| c) | interesting | | the |
| d) | beautiful | | the |
| e) | awful | | the |

●○○ 2. Fülle die Lücken mit dem richtigen Adjektiv. → Lösung S. 103

boring • expensive • interesting

a) That was the most ________________ book I've ever read!

b) I think maths is ________________ but geography is more ________________ .

c) London is one of the most ________________ places in Europe – everything costs a lot there.

●○○ 2. Ergänze die Sätze mit der richtigen Steigerung. → Lösung S. 103

a) That was ________________ (exciting) film I've ever seen!

b) I was nervous before the test but you were even ________________ (nervous).

c) Michael is ________________ (polite) but his brother is even ________________ (polite) – he always says "please" and "thank you".

d) "Star Wars" is ________________ (popular) film at the moment.

e) Is skiing ________________ (dangerous) than surfing?

## 3 Unregelmäßige Steigerung (*Irregular comparison*)

●○○ 1. Unregelmäßig gesteigerte Adjektive musst du auswendig kennen. Schreibe die Sätze um, wie in der Klammer nach dem Satz angegeben.

→ Lösung S. 104

a) John was first in the race, Melanie was second and Jenny was third. (good / runner)

*Jenny is a good runner. Melanie is a better runner.*

*John is the best runner.*

b) Amy is not a good singer. Angie is a terrible singer, and Liz is a really, really terrible singer! (bad)

*Amy is a* ______________________________

______________________________

c) My favourite food is chips, then pizza, then spaghetti with tomato sauce. (good)

*I think spaghetti with tomato sauce is* ______________________________

______________________________

d) Lucy's got 10 euros, Mia's got 15 euros and Katie's got 20 euros. (much)

*Lucy's got some money,* ______________________________

______________________________

e) I didn't like "The Peanuts Movie", I hated "Spectre" and I really hated "Star Wars"! (bad)

*I think "The Peanuts Movie" is* ______________________________

______________________________

f) There are 15 girls in Class 5a, 18 girls in Class 5b and 19 girls in 5c. (many)

*There are some* ______________________________

______________________________

## 4 Stützwort nach Adjektiven (*Prop word after adjectives*)

●○○ 1. Beantworte die Fragen und verwende dabei das Stützwort *one / ones*. → Lösung S. 104

a) Which pencil do you need? (red)

I need ______________________

b) Do you want this vanilla ice-cream? (strawberry)

No, ______________________

c) Which cookies did you make? (chocolate)

______________________

d) Would you like a hot drink? (cold)

No, ______________________

●○○ 2. Ersetze in der Frage das Nomen durch *one / ones*. → Lösung S. 104

a) The book is too difficult for me. Is there an easier book?

______________________

b) This chair is really hard! Is there a more comfortable chair?

______________________

c) Those shoes are too small. Have you got some bigger shoes?

______________________

d) These jeans are too expensive. Have you got some cheaper jeans?

______________________

## 5 Gemischte Formen (*Mixed forms*)

●○○ 1. Markiere die richtige Form. → Lösung S. 104

a) We have moved to a new house. It's ____________ than our old one.

☐ bigger ☐ more big ☐ more bigger

b) We stayed in the ____________ hotel in the city.

☐ expensivest ☐ more expensive ☐ most expensive

c) Mmm – this cake is ____________ than those biscuits!

☐ tastier ☐ more tastier ☐ most tasty

d) What is the ____________ country you've visited?

☐ hoter ☐ hotter ☐ hottest

e) A mobile phone is ____________ than a camera.

☐ usefuller ☐ more useful ☐ usefullest

f) Our school is one of the ____________ buildings in our town.

☐ older ☐ more older ☐ oldest

●○○ 2. Füge das Adjektiv ein, als *comparative* oder *superlative*. → Lösung S. 104

a) I am strong but my sister is __________________ . (strong)

b) The President is __________________ person in the USA. (important)

c) Liam is __________________ at English than Benjamin. (good)

d) What is __________________ country in Europe? (small)

e) I think flowers are __________________ than trees. (beautiful)

f) London is __________________ city in Britain. (busy)

g) Mrs Driscoll is __________________ teacher in our school. (nice)

h) Our cat is friendly and our dog is even __________________ ! (friendly)

## 6 Vergleich im Satz (*Sentences with comparison*)

●○○ 1. Schreibe Sätze aus Informationen der Tabelle. → Lösung S. 104

Mount Everest: 8,848 m
Zugspitze: 2,962 m
Munich: 850 years
River Thames: 380 km
The Empire State Building: 381 m
The Burj Khalifa: 829 m
Rome: 2,500 years
River Nile: 6,853 km

high • long • old • tall

a) *Mount Everest is higher than the Zugspitze.*
b) *The Zugspitze is not as*
c) *The River Nile*
d) *The River Thames*
e) ______
f) ______
g) ______
h) ______

●○○ 2. Schreibe die Sätze als Vergleich.
*as … as / … than / …* → Lösung S. 104

a) The green box weighs 10 kilos and the blue box weighs 10 kilos.

______

b) The black shirt is more expensive than the white one.

______

c) Lily is 13 and Marie is 13, too.

______

d) This exercise is more difficult than exercise 1.

______

## 1 Steigerung mit *-er / -est* (*Comparison with -er / -est*)

Übungen ab S. 97

1.

| | Grundform | 1. Steigerung | 2. Steigerung |
|---|---|---|---|
| a) | big | bigger | the biggest |
| b) | fast | faster | the fastest |
| c) | cold | colder | the coldest |
| d) | happy | happier | the happiest |
| e) | easy | easier | the easiest |

2.

| | Grundform | 1. Steigerung | 2. Steigerung |
|---|---|---|---|
| a) | clever | cleverer | the cleverest |
| b) | narrow | narrower | the narrowest |
| c) | simple | simpler | the cleverest |

3. The River Isar is **long** but the River Amazon is **longer**. b) Tom is the **youngest** boy in our class. c) Jenny tells great jokes – she's much **funnier** than you! d) I often work in the library. It's the **quietest** place in the school.

## 2 Steigerung mit *more / most* (*Comparison with more / most*)

Übungen ab S. 98

1.

| | Grundform | 1. Steigerung | 2. Steigerung |
|---|---|---|---|
| a) | boring | more boring | the most boring |
| b) | exciting | more exciting | the most exciting |
| c) | interesting | more interesting | the most interesting |
| d) | beautiful | more beautiful | the most beautiful |
| e) | awful | more awful | the most awful |

2. a) That was the most **interesting** book I've ever read! b) I think maths is **boring** but geography is more **boring**. c) London is one of the most **expensive** places in Europe – everything costs a lot there.

   b) That was **the most exciting** film I've ever seen! b) I was nervous before the test but you were even **more nervous**. c) Michael is **polite** but his brother is even **more polite** – he always says "please" and "thank you". d) "Star Wars" is **the most popular** film at the moment. e) Is skiing **more dangerous** than surfing?

## 3 Unregelmäßige Steigerung (*Irregular comparison*)

→ Übungen ab S. 99

1. b) Amy is a bad singer, Angie is a worse singer and Liz is the worst singer. c) I think spaghetti with tomato sauce is good, pizza is better and chips are the best. d) Lucy's got some money, Mia's got more money and Katie's got the most money. e) I think "The Peanuts Movie" is bad, "Spectre" is worse and "Star Wars" is the worst. f) There are some girls in Class 5a, more girls in Class 5b and the most girls in Class 5c.

## 4 Stützwort nach Adjektiven (*Prop word after adjectives*)

→ Übungen ab S. 100

1. a) I need the red one. b) No, I want the **strawberry one**. c) I made the **chocolate ones**. d) No, I'd like a **cold one**.

2. a) Is there an easier **one**? b) Is there a more comfortable **one**? c) Have you some bigger **ones**? d) Have you got some cheaper **ones**?

## 5 Gemischte Formen (*Mixed forms*)

→ Übungen ab S. 101

1. a) It's **bigger** than our old one. b) We stayed in the **most expensive** hotel in the city. c) Mmm – this cake is **tastier** than those biscuits! d) What is the **hottest** country you've visited? e) A mobile phone is **more useful** than a camera. f) Our school is one of the **oldest** buildings in our town.

2. a) I am strong but my sister is **stronger**. b) The President is the **most important** person in the USA. c) Liam is **better** at English than Benjamin. d) What is **the smallest** country in Europe? e) I think flowers are **more beautiful** than trees. f) London is **the busiest** city in Britain. g) Mrs Driscoll is **the nicest** teacher in our school. h) Our cat is friendly and dog is even **friendlier**!

## 6 Vergleich im Satz (*Sentences with comparison*)

→ Übungen ab S. 102

1. b) The Zugspitze is **not as high as** Mount Everest. c) The River Nile is **longer than** the River Thames. d) The River Thames is **not as long as** the River Nile. e) The Burj Khalifa is **higher than** the Empire State Building. f) The Empire State Building is **not as high as** the Burj Khalifa. g) Rome is **older than** Munich. h) Munich is **not as old as** Rome.

2. The green box is **as heavy as** the blue box. b) The white shirt is not **as expensive as / cheaper than** the black one. c) Lily is **as old as** Marie. d) Exercise 1 is not **as difficult as / easier than** this exercise.

# Adverbien der Art und Weise (*Adverbs of manner*)

## 1 Regelmäßige Formen (*Regular forms*)

●○○ 1. Adverbien beschreiben das Verb näher. Meistens hängst du einfach *-ly* an das entsprechende Adjektiv. → Lösung S. 109

aggressive • calm • hungry • loud • quick • slow

a) Wow! You finished your homework ____________ today!

b) My grandpa can't hear very well. You have to speak ____________ .

c) The dog ate its food ____________ .

d) Don't walk so ____________ ! Hurry up – we're late!

e) If the fire alarm rings, stand up and leave the building ____________ .

f) This match is unfair. The other team is playing too ____________ .

●●○ 2. Ändere die Sätze so, dass aus dem Adjektiv ein Adverb wird. Verwende dabei die Angaben in der Klammer. → Lösung S. 109

a) My mum is a careful driver. (drive)

*She drives carefully.*

b) Chris is a polite boy. (speak)

____________________________________________

c) Lena was very angry. (shout / at me)

____________________________________________

d) This exercise was easy. (I / do)

____________________________________________

e) The children were happy. (play)

____________________________________________

## 2 Unregelmäßige Formen (*Irregular forms*)

●○○ 1. Schreibe Sätze mit der Information aus der Tabelle. Verwandle die Adjektive in Adverbien. → Lösung S. 109

| | activity | adjective | person |
|---|---|---|---|
| a) | play guitar | good | Michael |
| b) | train | hard | the basketball team |
| c) | speak | friendly | the shop assistant |
| d) | run | fast | Katie |
| e) | dance | good | Andy |
| f) | work | hard | our class |
| g) | smile | friendly | Mr Matthews |

a) *Michael plays the guitar well.*

b) ____________________

c) ____________________

d) ____________________

e) ____________________

f) ____________________

g) ____________________

●○○ 2. Ergänze die Sätze mit *hard*, *fast* oder *well*. → Lösung S. 109

a) It's difficult to understand you when you speak so __________ .

b) If you want to play tennis __________ , you have to practise __________ .

c) I don't ski very __________ but I still enjoy it.

d) Don't eat so __________ ! You will be sick!

## 3 Steigerung der Adverbien (*Comparison of adverbs*)

●○○ 1. Füge die richtige Steigerung der Adverbien ein. → Lösung S. 109

a) You must listen ____________ when the teacher is talking! (careful)

b) The person who finishes ____________ can go home. (fast)

c) Phil is very aggressive. He should speak ____________. (polite)

d) Please drive ____________! This road is very dangerous! (slow)

e) Our dad cooks ____________ in our family – nobody likes his food! (bad)

f) We need to walk ____________ or we'll miss the train. (quick)

g) The sun is shining ____________ today than yesterday. (bright)

h) You can ride your bike ____________ if you wear a helmet. (safe)

●●○ 2. Übertrage die Sätze ins Englische. → Lösung S. 109

a) Helen arbeitet langsamer als Maria.

______________________________________________

b) Jamie fährt vorsichtiger als Caroline.

______________________________________________

c) Angela tanzt am schönsten.

______________________________________________

d) Du musst nicht schreien! Sprich bitte leiser!

______________________________________________

e) Tom schreibt viel schlechter als ich – ich kann das nicht lesen.

______________________________________________

## 4 Gemischte Formen (*Mixed forms*)

●○○ 1. Adjektiv oder Adverb? Was muss in die Lücke? → Lösung S. 109

a) Please walk ____________ ! The floor is wet.
☐ careful ☐ carefully

b) Emma answered all the questions ____________ .
☐ easy ☐ easily

c) I'm working ____________ today because I want to pass the test.
☐ hard ☐ hardly

d) Our dog is ____________ because he's getting quite old.
☐ slow ☐ slowly

e) Please talk ____________ – the baby is asleep.
☐ quiet ☐ quietly

f) Michelle ____________ helped me pack my bags.
☐ kind ☐ kindly

g) That's a ____________ photo! Did you take it?
☐ nice ☐ nicely

●○○ 2. Füge ein: Adjektiv: *good* oder Adverb: *well*. → Lösung S. 109

a) Rosanna speaks Spanish really ____________ .

b) Paul's English isn't very ____________ . I can't understand him.

c) Did you have a ____________ weekend?

d) My little sister can't talk very ____________ , but she's only two!

e) Judy's gone home because she isn't feeling ____________ .

f) The holiday was great but the weather wasn't very ____________ .

## 1 Regelmäßige Formen (*Regular forms*)

Übungen ab S. 105

1. a) Wow! You finished your homework **quickly** today! b) My grandpa can't hear very well. You have to speak **loudly**. c) The dog ate its food **hungrily**. d) Don't walk so **slowly**! Hurry up – we're late! e) If the fire alarm rings, stand up and leave the building **calmly**. g) This match is unfair. The other team is playing too **aggressively**.

2. b) He speaks politely. c) She shouted angrily at me. d) I did it easily. e) They played happily.

## 2 Unregelmäßige Formen (*Irregular forms*)

Übungen ab S. 106

1. b) The basketball team trains hard. c) The shop assistant spoke in a friendly way. d) Katie runs fast. e) Andy dances well. f) Our class works hard. g) Mr Matthews smiled in a friendly way.

2. a) It's difficult to understand you when you speak so **fast**. b) If you want to place tennis **well**, you have to practise **hard**. c) I don't ski very **well** but I still enjoy it. d) Don't eat so **fast**! You will be sick!

## 3 Steigerung der Adverbien (*Comparison of adverbs*)

Übungen ab S. 107

1. a) You must listen **more carefully** when the teacher is talking! b) The person who finishes **fastest** can go home. c) Phil is very aggressive. He should speak **more politely**. d) Please drive **more slowly**! This road is very dangerous! e) Our dad cooks **the worst** in our family – nobody likes his food! f) We need to walk **more quickly** or we'll miss the train. g) The sun is shining **more brightly** today than it was yesterday. h) You can ride your bike **more safely** if you wear a helmet.

2. a) Helen works more slowly than Maria. b) Jamie drives more carefully than Caroline. c) Angela dances the most beautifully. d) You don't need to shout! Please speak more quietly! e) Tom writes worse than me – I can't read this.

## 4 Gemischte Formen (*Mixed forms*)

Übungen ab S. 108

1. a) carefully b) easily c) hard d) slow e) quietly f) kindly g) nice

2. a) Rosanna speaks Spanish really **well**. b) Paul's English isn't very **good**. I can't understand him. c) Did you have a **good** weekend? d) My little sister can't talk very **well**, but she's only two! e) Judy's gone home because she isn't feeling **well**. f) The holiday was great but the weather wasn't very **good**.

# Possessivpronomen (*Possessive pronouns*)

## 1 Possessivpronomen (*Possessive pronouns*)

●○○ 1. Ersetze das unterstrichene Nomen durch *mine, yours, his, hers, ours, yours, theirs.*

→ Lösung S. 111

a) This isn't Pete's jacket. Pete's jacket is black, not blue.

This isn't Pete's jacket. His is black, not blue.

b) "Whose ball is this?" "It's my ball."

________________________________

c) My parents haven't got a dog now. Their dog died last year.

________________________________

d) That's my exercise book, not her exercise book.

________________________________

e) We live in a flat, too, but our flat is in the city centre.

________________________________

●○○ 2. Markiere die richtige Form.

→ Lösung S. 111

a) We bought a new map because we left __________ at the hotel.

☐ our ☐ ours

b) My cousins showed me __________ new hamster.

☐ their ☐ theirs

c) Don't drink that cola! It isn't __________ !

☐ your ☐ yours

d) d) Have you seen __________ English book?

☐ my ☐ mine

## 1 Possessivpronomen (*Possessive pronouns*)

→ Übungen ab S. 110

1. b) "Whose ball is this?" "It's **mine**." c) My parents haven't got a dog now. **Theirs** died last year. d) That's my exercise book, not **hers**. e) We live in a flat, too, but **ours** is in the city centre.

2. a) We bought a new map because we left **ours** at the hotel. b) My cousins showed me **their** new hamster. c) Don't drink that cola! It isn't **yours**! d) Have you seen **my** English book?

# *Have* und *have got*

## 1 *Have / have got*

●○○ 1. Schreibe die Sätze neu, ersetze *have / has* durch *have got / has got*.

→ Lösung S. 114

a) I have a new e-mail address.

J've got a new e-mail address.

b) Does the hotel have wi-fi?

________________________________________

c) They haven't got enough money for the tickets.

________________________________________

d) You have three new messages.

________________________________________

●○○ 2. Markiere die richtige Alternative.

→ Lösung S. 114

a) __________ a TV in your bedroom?

☐ Got you ☐ Have you got

b) No, I __________ a smartphone, but I want one.

☐ haven't got ☐ haven't

c) __________ a pet when he was young?

☐ Had Tommy ☐ Did Tommy have

d) It isn't fair! __________ three tests this week!

☐ We've got ☐ We got

e) I __________ a favourite band. I like different types of music.

☐ haven't ☐ haven't got

## 2 Gemischte Formen (*Mixed forms*)

●○○ 1. Schaue die Bilder an und beschreibe, was passiert.
Hier verwendest du nur *have*. → Lösung S. 114

breakfast • a coffee • fun • a shower

a) He's ______________________ b) They're ______________________

c) They're ______________________ d) I'm ______________________

●○○ 2. Kannst du hier beides verwenden – *have* und *have got*?
Wenn nicht, streiche durch, was falsch ist. → Lösung S. 114

a) We had / had got a great time at Paul's birthday party.

b) I usually have / have got a glass of warm milk before I go to bed.

c) Liam doesn't have / hasn't got time to meet us this afternoon.

d) Grandad has / has got a rest every day after lunch.

e) The children have / have got a bath in the evening.

f) My parents have / have got a new shower in their bathroom.

g) I'm hungry. Do you have / Have you got anything to eat?

## 1 *Have / have got*

→ Übungen ab S. 112

1. b) Has the hotel got wi-fi? c) They don't have enough money for the tickets. d) You've got/ You have got three new messages.

2. a) **Have you got** a TV in your bedroom? b) No, I **haven't got** a smartphone, but I want one. c) **Did Tommy have** a pet when he was young? d) It isn't fair! **We've got** three tests this week! e) I **haven't got** a favourite band. I like different types of music.

## 2 Gemischte Formen (*Mixed forms*)

→ Übungen ab S. 113

1. a) He's having a shower. b) They're having breakfast. c) They're having fun. d) I'm having a coffee.

2. b) I usually **have** / ~~**have got**~~ a glass of warm milk before I go to bed. c) Liam doesn't **have** / **hasn't** got time to meet us this afternoon. d) Grandad **has** / ~~**has got**~~ a rest every day after lunch. e) The children **have** / ~~**have got**~~ a bath in the evening. f) My parents **have** / **have got** a new shower in their bathroom. g) I'm hungry. **Do** you **have** / **Have** you **got** anything to eat?

# Wortstellung (*Word order*)

## 1 S – V – O (*subject – verb – object*)

●○○ 1. Bilde aus den Wörtern Sätze mit richtiger Wortstellung.

→ Lösung S. 117

a) door / closed / Jack / the

______________________________

b) me / text / Joanne / a / sends/ often

______________________________

c) do / after / homework / I / my / school

______________________________

d) home / came / the / when / his / on / mother / Danny / sleeping / sofa.

______________________________

e) can / piano / my / sister / play / the

______________________________

●●○ 2. Übertrage ins Englische.

→ Lösung S. 117

a) Ich spiele am Samstag immer Volleyball.

______________________________

b) Wenn sie Hunger hat, isst Maria gerne Obst.

______________________________

c) Du kannst sehr gut Französisch sprechen.

______________________________

d) Wir sehen immer am Wochenende viel fern.

______________________________

## 2 Stellung von Adverbien (*Position of adverbs*)

●○○ 1. Ist die Wortstellung im Satz richtig? Korrigiere. → Lösung S. 117

a) Tom has breakfast usually in a café.

______________________________

b) We saw yesterday a good film at the cinema.

______________________________

c) They go always to the USA on holiday.

______________________________

d) Did you go for a swim last weekend in the lake?

______________________________

e) Please go back after break to your classroom.

______________________________

●○○ 2. Ergänze die Sätze mit einer Orts- und einer Zeitangabe. → Lösung S. 117

at home / today • here / since June 2015 • in his favourite • armchair / after dinner • at school / yesterday • outside the • cinema / at 7 o'clock • to the concert / next week

a) Annie arrived late ______________________________

b) We have lived ______________________________

c) Are you going ______________________________

d) We're meeting ______________________________

e) Grandpa sits ______________________________

f) Alex is ill, so he's staying ______________________________

## 1 S – V – O (*subject* – *verb* – object)

→ Übungen ab S. 115

1. a) Jack closed the door. b) Joanne often sends me a text. c) I do my homework after school. d) When his mother came home, Danny was sleeping on the sofa. e) My sister can play the piano.

2. a) I always play volleyball on Saturday. b) When she is hungry, Maria likes to eat fruit. c) You can speak French very well. d) We always watch a lot of TV at the weekend.

## 2 Stellung von Adverbien (*Position of adverbs*)

→ Übungen ab S. 116

1. a) Tom usually has breakfast in a café. b) We saw a good film at the cinema yesterday. c) They always go to the USA on holiday. d) Did you go for a swim in the lake last weekend? e) Please go back to your classroom after break.

2. a) Annie arrived late **at school yesterday**. b) We have lived **here since June 2015**. c) Are you going **to the concert next week**? d) We're meeting **outside the cinema at 7 o'clock**. e) Grandpa sits **in his favourite armchair after dinner**. f) Alex is ill, so he's staying **at home today**.

# Zusammensetzungen von *some* und *any* (*Compounds of "some" and "any"*)

## 1 *somebody / someone* oder *anybody / anyone*

●○○ 1. Ergänze *somebody / someone* oder *anybody / anyone*. → Lösung S. 121

a) ____________ has just sent me a message.

b) Hello? Can ____________ hear me?

c) That's not fair! ____________ has eaten all the cake!

d) ____________ gave me this book for my birthday.

e) There isn't ____________ in the classroom.

f) ____________ is playing very loud music!

g) Does ____________ know what the German homework is?

●○○ 2. Schreibe die Sätze um, so dass du das jeweils andere Wort einsetzen musst: *someone / anyone*. → Lösung S. 121

a) There's someone in the kitchen.

There isn't anyone in the kitchen.

b) We didn't see anyone.

____________

c) I helped someone last week.

____________

d) Greg didn't tell anyone what happened.

____________

e) They met someone nice on holiday.

____________

## 2 *something / anything* und *somewhere / anywhere*

●○○ 1. Ergänze *something* oder *anything*. → Lösung S. 121

a) "What did you say?" "I didn't say anything ______."

b) "Did you break this glass?" "No, I didn't break ______."

c) "Did Lucy tell you where we're going?" "Yes, she told me ______ but I don't remember what she said."

d) "What did you have for lunch?" "I didn't eat ______."

e) "Shall we watch this film?" "Yes, I'd like to watch ______."

f) "Did you buy ______ in town?"

g) "Was the test easy?" "No! I didn't understand ______."

h) "Did Paul help you clean up?" "No, he didn't do ______."

●○○ 2. Markiere das richtige Wort. → Lösung S. 121

a) Zoe lives ______ near you, doesn't she?
☐ somewhere ☐ anywhere

b) I've lost my phone! I can't find it ______!
☐ somewhere ☐ anywhere

c) Are you going ______ on holiday this summer?
☐ somewhere ☐ anywhere

d) "Where's the new shoe shop?" "It's ______ in the city centre."
☐ somewhere ☐ anywhere

e) It's too hot here. I want to sit ______ else.
☐ somewhere ☐ anywhere

## 3 Gemischte Formen (*Mixed forms*)

●○○ 1. Verbinde die Satzhälften, die zusammenpassen. → Lösung S. 121

| | |
|---|---|
| a) I'm thirsty. I'd like | Somebody has taken mine! |
| b) They say King Arthur lived | I've got too much homework. |
| c) Has anyone seen | something to drink. |
| d) Sean doesn't eat | in my room. It must be at school. |
| e) This isn't my jacket! | something in my eye. |
| f) The book isn't anywhere | our dog? We can't find him! |
| g) Does anyone want to go | anything with cheese in it. |
| h) I can't go anywhere today: | something about China. |
| i) Today we learned | somewhere near this mountain. |
| j) I can't see! There's | to the cinema with me? |

●●○ 2. Ergänze die Lücken. → Lösung S. 121

a) Have you got ____________________ to eat? I'm really hungry!

b) Their house is ____________________ near the river.

c) This room stinks! I think ____________________ has been smoking in here.

d) The children are bored. They haven't got ____________________ to do.

e) Little Jamie doesn't go ____________________ without his teddy bear.

f) I want to buy ____________________ new to wear for Emma's party.

g) We are looking for ____________________ to train the under-12s football team.

h) There isn't ____________________ to play in this street.

## 1 *somebody / someone / anybody / anyone*

Übungen ab S. 118

1. a) **Somebody** has just sent me a message. b) Hello? Can **anybody** hear me? c) That's not fair! **Somebody** has eaten all the cake! d) **Somebody** gave me this book for my birthday. e) There isn't **anybody** in the classroom. f) **Somebody** is playing very loud music! g) Does **anybody** know what the German homework is?

2. b) We saw someone. c) I didn't help anyone last week. d) Greg told someone what happened. e) They didn't meet anyone nice on holiday.

## 2 *something / anything* und *somewhere / anywhere*

Übungen ab S. 119

1. b) "Did you break this glass?" "No, I didn't break **anything**". c) "Did Lucy tell you where we're going?" "Yes, she told me **something** but I don't remember what she said." d) "What did you have for lunch?" "I didn't eat **anything**." e) "Shall we watch this film?" "Yes, I'd like to watch **something**." f) "Did you buy **anything** in town?" g) "Was the test easy?" "No! I didn't understand **anything**." h) "Did Paul help you clean up?" "No, he didn't do **anything**."

2. a) Zoe lives **somewhere** near you, doesn't she? b) I've lost my phone! I can't find it **anywhere**! c) Are you going **anywhere** on holiday this year? d) "Where's the new shoe shop?" "It's **somewhere** in the city centre." e) It's too hot here. I want to sit **somewhere** else.

## 3 Gemischte Formen (*Mixed forms*)

Übungen ab S. 120

1. a) I'm thirsty. I'd like something to drink. b) They say King Arthur lived somewhere near this mountain. c) Has anyone seen our dog? We can't find him! d) Sean doesn't eat anything with cheese in it. e) This isn't my jacket! Somebody has taken mine! f) The book isn't anywhere in my room. It must be at school. g) Does anyone want to go to the cinema with me? h) I can't go anywhere this evening: I've got too much homework. i) Today we learned something about China. j) I can't see! There's something in my eye.

2. a) Have you got **anything** to eat? I'm really hungry! b) Their house is **somewhere** near the river. c) This room stinks! I think **someone / somebody** has been smoking in here. d) The children are bored. They haven't got **anything** to do. e) Little Jamie doesn't **anywhere** without his teddy bear. f) I want to buy **something** new to wear for Emma's party. g) We are looking for **someone / somebody** to train the under-12s football team. h) There isn't **anywhere** to play in this street.

# Zusammensetzungen mit *every* und *no* (*Compounds of "every" and "no"*)

## 1 *everything / everyone / everybody / everywhere*

●○○ 1. Verbinde die Satzteile, die zusammenpassen. → Lösung S. 124

| | |
|---|---|
| a) Can everybody please | he likes everyone! |
| b) Have you got everything | and go outside. |
| c) They looked everywhere | sit down and be quiet! |
| d) There's no food! My brothers | everywhere after the storm. |
| e) Our dog is very friendly: | you need for your holiday? |
| f) Leave everything on your desk | for the missing bags. |
| g) Joanne had a really big party: | have eaten everything! |
| h) There were broken trees | she invited everyone she knows. |

●●○ 2. Übersetze die Sätze ins Deutsche. → Lösung S. 124

a) They lost everything in the fire.

______________________________

b) I have looked everywhere for my keys.

______________________________

c) Has everybody got a pen?

______________________________

d) We put everything in the kitchen.

______________________________

e) There were toys everywhere!

______________________________

## 2 *nothing / no-one / nobody / nowhere*

●○○ 1. Markiere die richtige Zusammensetzung von *no*. → Lösung S. 124

a) "Who did you text yesterday?" "________ . I forgot my phone."

☐ Nobody ☐ Nothing ☐ Nowhere

b) "Where did you go on Saturday?" "________ . We stayed at home."

☐ Nobody ☐ Nothing ☐ Nowhere

c) We need to go to the supermarket. There's ________ to eat.

☐ nobody ☐ nothing ☐ nowhere

d) Erik is really unfriendly. ________ likes him.

☐ Nobody ☐ Nothing ☐ Nowhere

e) "What did they have for breakfast?" "________ . They weren't hungry."

☐ Nobody ☐ Nothing ☐ Nowhere

●●○ 2. Sind die Sätze richtig? Falls nicht, verbessere sie. → Lösung S. 124

a) They told anyone about the party.

______________________________

b) There's nothing good on TV this evening.

______________________________

c) I don't know what happened. She didn't tell me nothing.

______________________________

d) Sina's going anywhere today because she's feeling ill.

______________________________

e) Anybody saw her go into the house.

______________________________

# Zusammensetzungen mit *every* und *no* (*Compounds of "every" and "no"*)

## 1 *everything / everyone / everybody / everywhere*

→ Übungen ab S. 122

1. a) Can everybody please sit down and be quiet! b) Have you got everything you need for your holiday? c) They looked everywhere for the missing bags. d) There's no food! My brothers have eaten everything! e) Our dog is very friendly: he likes everyone! f) Leave everything on your desk and go outside. g) Joanne had a really big party: she invited everyone she knows. h) There were broken trees everywhere after the storm

2. a) Sie haben in dem Feuer alles verloren. b) Ich habe meine Schlüssel überall gesucht. c) Hat jeder einen Stift? d) Wir haben alles in der Küche gestellt. e) Es war überall Spielzeug! / Überall war Spielzeug!

## 2 *nothing / no-one / nobody / nowhere*

→ Übungen ab S. 123

1. a) Nobody b) Nowhere c) nothing d) Nobody e) Nothing

2. a) They **told no-one / didn't tell anyone** about the party. b) ✓ c) I don't know what happened. She **told me nothing / didn't tell me anything**. d) **Sina's going nowhere / Sina isn't going anywhere** today because she's feeling ill. e) **Nobody** saw her go into the house.

# Modale Hilfsverben (*Modal auxiliaries*)

## 1 *may / can / could / shall*

●○○ 1. Wie formell sind diese Sätze? Ergänze die Tabelle. → Lösung S. 132

| nicht formell | etwas formeller | formell |
|---|---|---|
| a) | | |
| | | |

a) Can I have a drink, please?

b) Yes, you may go now.

c) Could you give a message to Mrs Maloney?

d) May I have some more cake?

e) OK, you can sit here.

f) Could we order some food now, please?

●○○ 2. Schreibe Fragen mit shall, die zu den Antworten passen. → Lösung S. 132

a) Shall we go swimming today? – Yes, let's go swimming.

b) ______________________ – Yes, let's have a pizza.

c) ______________________ – No, I don't like ice-skating.

d) ______________________ – Yes, please help me with my homework.

e) ______________________ – Yes, we can meet at 5 o'clock.

f) ______________________ – No, I don't want to watch TV.

g) ______________________ – Yes, please send me Phil's phone number.

## 2 *can / be able to*

●○○ 1. Bringe die Sätze in eine andere Zeitform. Entweder in die Vergangenheit oder in der Zukunft. Verwende dabei eine Form von *be able to*.

→ Lösung S. 132

a) I can sleep late on Saturday morning.

Last Saturday morning *I was able to sleep late.*

b) We can meet in the afternoon.

__________ tomorrow.

c) John can finish all the exercises.

__________ yesterday.

d) I can't visit Charlie today.

__________ next week.

e) We have to go now. We can't wait any longer.

We had to go yesterday. We __________

●○○ 2. Füge eine Form von *be able to* und ein Verb ein.

→ Lösung S. 132

go • find • ski • speak • walk

a) After he finished the language course, Andy

__________ much better Spanish.

b) Yes, I __________ to the cinema with you next weekend.

c) They live in the mountains and __________ when they were three years old!

d) Ben broke his leg and __________ for six weeks.

e) Look on the internet. You __________ the information there.

## 3 *can / may / be allowed to*

●○○ 1. Welche Regeln gelten im Bus – schreibe Fragen und Antworten mit den Stichwörtern. → Lösung S. 132

**Rules for the school bus**

- No food or drink!
- Sit down when the bus is moving!
- Do not speak to the driver when the bus is moving!
- No shouting or singing!

a) eat / drink?

*May/Can we eat and drink on the bus? – No, you're not allowed to.*

b) stand up / bus / moving?

_______________

c) speak / driver / at bus stop?

_______________

d) talk / quietly / to / friends?

_______________

●○○ 2. Bilde aus den angegebenen Wörtern richtige Sätze. → Lösung S. 132

a) will / to / have / they / allowed / be / ice-cream / an

_______________

b) stay / wasn't / to / allowed / I / late / up

_______________

c) allowed / we / go / were / out / to

_______________

## 4 *be able to* und *be allowed to*

●○○ 1. Markiere die beste Lösung. → Lösung S. 132

a) Tom ____________ play computer games after 8 p.m.

☐ isn't allowed to ☐ isn't able to

b) If it is hot next week, we ____________ go swimming in the lake.

☐ won't be allowed to ☐ will be able to

c) I ____________ ride a bike when I was four years old.

☐ was allowed to ☐ was able to

d) ____________ take photos in the museum?

☐ Will we be allowed to ☐ Will we be able to

e) She ____________ find all the missing information.

☐ wasn't allowed to ☐ was able to

●●○ 2. Füge *able to* oder *allowed to* in die Lücken ein. → Lösung S. 132

I love Wednesdays! That's the day my mum works late, and so I go to my grandma's after school. It's great at grandma's house! First of all, I'm ________________ watch TV before I start my homework. I am ________________ do that at home, because mum says I won't be ________________ concentrate on my homework afterwards. Another good thing is that grandma lived in England for many years. That means she is ________________ help me with my English homework.
After homework, I'm ________________ chat online with my friends and play a couple of games on my phone. Then I go into the kitchen for some homemade cake, warm from the oven. I hope I'll be ________________ go to grandma's every week this year!

## 5 *must / mustn't / needn't / have to / don't have to*

●○○ 1. Schreibe die Sätze neu, verwende *must* oder *have to*. → Lösung S. 133

a) We must leave at 3 o'clock.

We have to leave at 3 o'clock.

b) He has to mend his bike.

______________________________

c) Must I go with you?

______________________________

d) You have to learn these words.

______________________________

e) Does Mark have to clean his room?

______________________________

●○○ 2. Bringe die Sätze in die Vergangenheit oder in die Zukunft.
Vorsicht: dadurch ändert sich das modale Hilfsverb. → Lösung S. 133

a) I must get up early.

I will have to get up early tomorrow.

b) We needn't read the book this week.

______________________________ last week.

c) Molly must walk her dog every day.

______________________________ yesterday.

d) Must we wait for Caroline?

______________________________ tomorrow morning?

e) They needn't go to football training today.

______________________________ next Saturday.

●○○ 3. Füge das passende modale Hilfsverb ein. Du brauchst: *mustn't* oder *don't / doesn't have to*. → Lösung S. 133

a) We ________________ talk when we are taking a test.

b) I ________________ do my homework now. I can do it tomorrow.

c) You ________________ eat this if you don't like it.

d) Claire ________________ forget to send me the e-mail.

e) Alex ________________ come with us if he doesn't want to.

f) They ________________ use their phones in the classroom.

g) I ________________ help you. You have to do it alone.

h) Bill Gates is a billionaire. He ________________ look for a job.

i) You ________________ tell Katie about the present – it's a surprise!

●●○ 4. Sind diese Sätze richtig? Wenn nicht, verbessere sie. → Lösung S. 133

a) You mustn't go by train into town. You can walk from here.

________________________________________

b) We had a pizza in town so we needn't to cook anything now.

________________________________________

c) It's Saturday! We don't have to go to school!

________________________________________

d) I mustn't go to the library. I can find the information online.

________________________________________

e) You haven't to wear a jacket. It isn't cold today.

________________________________________

f) What time is it? We mustn't be late!

________________________________________

## 6 *should / shouldn't*

●○○ 1. Schreibe Sätze mit *should* oder *shouldn't*, ein Verb und den Stichwörtern. → Lösung S. 133

a) You ______________________________
(too much / TV)

b) You ______________________________
(every day)

c) You ______________________________
(mobile / in class)

●○○ 2. Füge *should* oder *shouldn't* in die Lücken ein. → Lösung S. 133

a) You ______________ eat so much chocolate.

b) I ______________ write the new words in my vocabulary book.

c) We ______________ travel by car so much. We ______________ ride our bikes more.

d) If you feel sick, you ______________ stay at home.

e) The children ______________ wear their hats. It's very cold outside.

f) Len ______________ drink so much coffee in the evening!

g) We ______________ be careful when we surf the internet.

h) You ______________ be polite to your teachers.

## 1 *may / can / could / shall*

Übungen ab S. 125

1. nicht formell: a), e); etwas formeller: c), f); formell: b), d)

2. b) Shall we have a pizza? c) Shall we go ice-skating? d) Shall I help you with your homework? e) Shall we meet at 5 o'clock? f) Shall we watch TV? g) Shall I send you Phil's phone number?

## 2 *can / be able to*

Übungen ab S. 126

1. b) We **will be able to** meet in the afternoon tomorrow. c) John **was able to** finish all the exercises yesterday. d) I **won't be able to** visit Charlie next week. e) We had to go yesterday. We **weren't able to** wait any longer.

2. a) After he finished the language course, Andy **was able to speak** much better Spanish. b) Yes, I **will be able to go** to the cinema with you next weekend. c) They live in the mountains and **were able to ski** when they were three years old! d) Ben broke his leg and **wasn't able to walk** for six weeks. e) Look on the internet. You **will be able to find** the information there.

## 3 *can / may / be allowed to*

Übungen ab S.127

1. b) May / Can we stand up when the bus is moving? – No, you're not allowed to. c) May / Can we speak to the driver at a bus stop? – Yes, you're allowed to. d) May / Can we talk quietly to our friends? – Yes, you're allowed to.

2. a) They will be allowed to have an ice-cream. b) I wasn't allowed to stay up late. c) We were allowed to go out.

## 4 *be able to* und *be allowed to*

Übungen ab S. 128

1. a) Tom **isn't allowed to** play computer games after 8 p.m. b) If it is hot next week, we **will be able to** go swimming in the lake. c) I **was able to** ride a bike when I was four years old. d) **Will we be allowed to** take photos in the museum? e) She **was able to** find all the missing information.

2. I love Wednesdays! That's the day my mum works late, and so I go to my grandma's after school. It's great at grandma's house! First of all, I'm **allowed to** watch TV before I start my homework. I am **not allowed to** do that at home, because mum says I won't be **able to** concentrate on my homework afterwards. Another good thing is that grandma lived in England for many years. That means she is **able to** help me with my English homework. After homework, I'm **allowed to** chat online with my friends and play a couple of games on my phone. Then I go into the kitchen for some homemade cake, warm from the oven. I hope I'll be **able to** go to grandma's every week this year!

## 5 *must / mustn't / needn't / have to / don't have to*

Übungen ab S. 129

1. b) He **must** mend his bike. c) **Do** I **have to** go with you? d) You **must** learn these words. e) **Must** Mark clean his room?

2. b) We **didn't have to** read the book last week. c) Molly **had to walk** her dog yesterday. d) **Will** we **have to** wait for Caroline tomorrow morning? e) They **won't have to** go to football training next Saturday.

3. a) We **mustn't** talk when we are taking a test. b) I **don't have to** do my homework now. I can do it tomorrow. c) You **don't have to** eat this if you don't like it. d) Claire **mustn't** forget to send me the e-mail. e) Alex **doesn't have to** come with us if he doesn't want to. f) They **mustn't** use their phones in the classroom. g) I **mustn't** help you. You have to do it alone. h) Bill Gates is a billionaire. He **doesn't have to** look for a job. i) You **mustn't** tell Katie about the present – it's a surprise!

4. a) You **don't have to** go by train to town. b) We had a pizza in town so we **needn't / don't have to** cook anything now. c) ✓ d) I **don't have to** go to the library. I can find the information online. e) You **don't have to / needn't** wear a jacket. It isn't cold today. f) ✓

## 6 *should / shouldn't*

Übungen ab S. 131

1. a) You **shouldn't watch** too much TV. b) You **should clean** your teeth every day. c) You **shouldn't use** your mobile in class.

2. a) You **shouldn't** eat so much chocolate. b) I **should** write the new words in my vocabulary book. c) We **shouldn't** travel by car so much. We **should** ride our bikes more. d) If you feel sick, you **should** stay at home. e) The children **should** wear their hats. It's very cold outside. f) Len **shouldn't** drink so much coffee in the evening! g) We **should** be careful when we surf the internet. h) You **should** be polite to your teachers.

# Bedingungssätze (*Conditional sentences*)

## 1 Bedingungssätze Typ I (*Conditional sentences type I*)

●○○ 1. Verbinde die Satzhälften, die zusammenpassen. → Lösung S. 138

| | |
|---|---|
| a) If you lose this book, | have something to eat. |
| b) They'll get into trouble | if there's enough snow. |
| c) If I don't write down the new words | you'll have to buy me a new one. |
| d) We'll go skiing this weekend | I won't remember them. |
| e) If Jeff trains harder | if they use their phones in class. |
| f) Our team can win | I'll send you the link. |
| g) If you are hungry, | if they don't go to sleep soon. |
| h) If you want to watch the video | if they score another goal. |
| i) The children will be tired | he'll be able to run faster. |

●○○ 2. Füge die richtige Form der Verben in die Lücken ein. → Lösung S. 138

a) If I ____________ (have) time, I ____________ (go) for a run this evening.

b) If it ____________ (rain) this afternoon, we ____________ (stay) at home.

c) You ____________ (be) late if you ____________ (not/get up) now!

d) ____________ (tell) the police if you ____________ (see) a thief!

e) If they ____________ (need) any help, they ____________ (can/ask) me.

f) Maria ____________ (come) to the party if we ____________ (invite) her.

g) If I ____________ (eat) this too fast, I ____________ (get) sick.

h) If you ____________ (be) so tired, just ____________ (go) to bed.

●●○ 3. Verbessere die Fehler in diesen Sätzen. → Lösung S. 138

a) If you will see Cathy tomorrow, please say hello from me.

______________________________

b) My parents will buy a new car if they will have enough money.

______________________________

c) If we won't leave now, we will miss the train.

______________________________

d) If you like exciting movies, you enjoy the new "Star Wars" film!

______________________________

e) The cat is hungry if you won't feed it.

______________________________

●●○ 4. Bilde aus den angegebenen Wörtern richtige Sätze, verwende *if* und die richtigen Verbformen. → Lösung S. 138

a) be / sunny / this afternoon / we / play / outside

*If it's sunny this afternoon, we'll play outside.*

b) you / like / cats / you / love / this video

______________________________

c) I / not know / answer / I / ask / Mrs Stewart

______________________________

d) she / speak / slowly / we / understand / her

______________________________

e) we / not hurry / we / not have / time / for lunch

______________________________

## 2 *If* oder *when*

●○○ 1. Werden diese Ereignisse ganz sicher eintreten oder nur vielleicht?

→ Lösung S. 138

a) When the lesson ends, we'll go outside and play table tennis.

☐ yes ☐ maybe

b) Please tell me the answer if you know it!

☐ yes ☐ maybe

c) I'll text Tina when I get home.

☐ yes ☐ maybe

d) If we go to a café later, my dad will pay for our drinks.

☐ yes ☐ maybe

●○○ 2. Setze *if* oder *when* in die Lücken.

→ Lösung S. 138

a) ____________ we finish this chapter, our teacher will give us a test.

b) ____________ Mum gets home, I'll tell her about the broken window!

c) ____________ you like this photo, I'll send it to you.

d) ____________ we have enough money, we'll got to Italy in the summer.

e) ____________ I get up tomorrow, I'll have a shower.

f) ____________ lots of people buy his CD, he'll soon be rich!

g) ____________ they can get tickets, they'll go to the concert.

h) ____________ we go on our class trip next week, we'll need to take sandwiches.

i) ____________ this film finishes, I'll go upstairs and clean my teeth.

j) ____________ they don't have any fish at the restaurant, I'll order pasta.

## 3 Bedingungssätze Typ II (*Conditional sentences type II*)

●○○ 1. Was gehört in die Lücken? Kreuze an. → Lösung S. 139

a) If I ____________ some cents on the street, I'd keep them.

☐ would find ☐ found

b) Karen would play guitar in our band if she ____________ more time.

☐ had ☐ has

c) You ____________ better if you drank less cola.

☐ felt ☐ would feel

d) If we ____________ now, we would have more time for shopping.

☐ would leave ☐ left

●○○ 2. Vervollständige den Text mit den richtigen Zeitformen der angegebenen Verben. → Lösung S. 139

I live with my parents in the middle of a big city. Some people would love that but I don't – I want to live in the country. If we ________________ (live) in the country, we ________________ (have) a big garden. If we ________________ (have) a big garden, we ________________ (get) a dog. If we ________________ (get) a dog, I ________________ (feed) it and look after it. But that's not all. I'm sure I ________________ (ride) my bike everywhere if we ________________ (move) to the country. Here in the city, where we live now, it is too dangerous to ride a bike on the roads. There are just too many cars and lorries. But not everything is bad in the city. My dad said that the internet connection is not always good in the countryside. Hmm – if I ________________ (not/can) go online all the time, I ________________ (not/be) very happy!

## 1 Bedingungssätze Typ I (*Conditional sentences type I*)

Übungen ab S. 134

1. a) If you lose this book, you'll have to buy me a new one. b) They'll get into trouble if they use their phones in class. c) If I don't write down the new words, I won't remember them. d) We'll go skiing this weekend if there's enough snow. e) If Jeff trains harder, he'll be able to run faster. f) Our team can win if they score another goal. g) If you are hungry, have something to eat. h) If you want to watch the video, I'll send you the link. i) The children will be tired if they don't go to sleep soon.

2. a) If I **have** time, I **will go** for a run this evening. b) If it **rains** this afternoon, we **will stay** at home. c) You **will be** late if you **don't get up** now! d) **Tell** the police if you **see** a thief! e) If they **need** any help, they **can ask** me. f) Maria **will come** to the party if we **invite her**. g) If I **eat** this too fast, I **will get** sick. h) If you **are** so tired, just **go** to bed.

3. a) If you **see** Cathy tomorrow, please say hello from me. b) My parents will buy a new car if they **have** enough money. c) If we **don't leave** now, we will miss the train. d) If you like exciting movies, you **will enjoy** the new "Star Wars" film! e) The cat **will be** hungry if you **don't feed** it.

4. b) If you like cats, you'll love this video. c) If I don't know the answer, I'll ask Mrs Stewart. d) If she speaks slowly, we'll understand her. e) If we don't hurry, we won't have time for lunch.

## 2 *If* oder *when*

Übungen ab S. 136

1. a) yes b) maybe c) yes d) maybe

2. a) **When** we finish this chapter, our teacher will give us a test. b) **When** Mum gets home, I'll tell her about the broken window! c) **If** you like this photo, I'll send it to you. d) **If** we have enough money, we'll go to Italy in the summer. e) **When** I get up tomorrow, I'll have a shower. f) **If** lots of people buy his CD, he'll soon be rich! g) **If** they can get tickets, they'll go to the concert. h) **When** we go on our class trip next week, we'll need to take sandwiches. j) **When** this film finishes, I'll go upstairs and clean my teeth. j) **If** they don't have any fish at the restaurant, I'll order pasta.

## 3 Bedingungssätze Typ II (*Conditional sentences type II*)

Übungen ab S. 137

1. a) If I **found** some cents on the street, I'd keep them. b) Karen would play guitar in our band if she **had** more time. c) You **would feel** better if you drank less cola. d) If we **left** now, we would have more time for shopping.

2. I live with my parents in the middle of a big city. Some people would love that but I don't – I want to live in the country. If we **lived** in the country, we **would have** a big garden. If we **had** a big garden, we **would get** a dog. If we **got** a dog, I **would feed** it and look after it. But that's not all. I'm sure I **would ride** my bike everywhere if we **moved** to the country. Here in the city, where we live now, it is too dangerous to ride a bike on the roads. There are just too many cars and lorries. But not everything is bad in the city. My dad said that the internet connection is not always good in the countryside. Hmm – if I **couldn't** go online all the time, I **would not be** very happy!

# Relativsätze (*Relative clauses*)

## 1 *who, which, that, whose*

●○○ 1. Füge das richtige Relativpronomen ein.
Du benötigst *who*, *which* oder *that*. → Lösung S. 144

a) I know someone ____________ can speak Chinese.

b) These are the photos ____________ Liam took on holiday.

c) That's the house ____________ I lived in when I was two.

d) Jenny is the girl ____________ sits next to me in the maths lesson.

e) Some people ____________ saw the film didn't like it.

f) The tree ____________ was in our garden fell down in the storm.

g) The cakes ____________ my aunt makes taste really good!

h) The book ____________ I'm reading is about horses.

●○○ 2. Markiere das richtige Pronomen: *who* oder *whose*. → Lösung S. 144

a) Juliet is the girl who / whose Romeo loved.

b) Is Pete the boy who / whose dad is a policeman?

c) The boys who / whose band is playing this evening go to my school.

d) They are looking for someone who / whose can help train the basketball team.

e) What's the name of the actor who / whose stars in that film?

f) The children who / whose ball was in our garden live in our street.

g) The pupils who / whose classroom is next to ours are always noisy.

h) Diana is my friend who / whose comes from Norwich.

## 2 Relativsätze mit Relativpronomen (*Relative clauses with relative pronouns*)

●○○ 1. Bilde aus den beiden Sätzen einen langen Satz. Verbinde sie mit dem richtigen Relativpronomen. → Lösung S. 144

a) I saw a woman. She was wearing green shoes.

*I saw a woman who/that was wearing green shoes.*

b) Bill bought a new phone. The phone was very expensive.

__________

c) The teacher asked me a question. The question was easy to answer.

__________

d) Charlotte is my friend. I met her on holiday last year.

__________

e) Japanese is a language. It is difficult to learn Japanese.

__________

●●○ 2. Verbessere die falschen Pronomen. → Lösung S. 144

a) Football is a sport what a lot of people enjoy.

__________

b) Who is the singer which sings "Hello"?

__________

c) I've got a computer who is very slow.

__________

d) A vegetarian is a person whose doesn't eat meat.

__________

## 3 Relativsätze ohne Relativpronomen (*Contact clauses*)

●○○ 1. Verbinde die beiden passenden Satzteile und setze nur dann *who*, *which* oder *that* ein, wo es nötig ist. → Lösung S. 144

| | | |
|---|---|---|
| a) The people | ___________ | has no shops and no schools. |
| b) Here's the book | ___________ | I've ever eaten! |
| c) I didn't see the message | ___________ | we met on holiday were nice. |
| d) They won the last match | ___________ | is talking to Sam is his friend. |
| e) This is the best pizza | ___________ | you wanted to read. |
| f) The hotel | ___________ | you gave her? |
| g) The boy | | was on my phone. |
| h) We live in a village | ___________ | took place on that day. |
| i) Did she like the present | ___________ | we stayed at was in Leeds. |

●●○ 2. Bilde Relativsätze ohne Relativpronomen. Lasse dazu die *schräg* gedruckten Wörter weg. → Lösung S. 144

a) I like the green jacket. She's wearing *it* today.

_______________________________________________

b) The musicians played very loud music. We listened to *them*.

_______________________________________________

c) The boy was Frank's brother. We saw *him* yesterday.

_______________________________________________

d) The number was wrong. You gave *it* to me.

_______________________________________________

## 4 Gemischte Formen (*Mixed forms*)

●○○ 1. Brauchst du hier das Relativpronomen unbedingt? Wenn nicht, streiche es durch. → Lösung S. 145

a) Tony was the first friend that I had at my new school.

b) A doctor is someone who helps sick people.

c) The woman who we spoke to was very friendly.

d) Fiona told me a story that was very interesting.

e) A fish is an animal which lives in water.

f) The flowers which I bought are for my mum.

g) The man that I sat next to on the plane was from New York.

h) Chocolate is something that many people like to eat.

i) A baker is a person who sells bread and cakes.

●●○ 2. Mache aus den zwei Sätzen einen. Überlege, ob du ein Relativpronomen brauchst oder nicht. → Lösung S. 145

a) I have a friend called Kate. She is my best friend.

_______________

b) There's a dog. The dog barks all night.

_______________

c) We learned some new vocabulary. The vocabulary was in our book.

_______________

d) She usually catches a bus. The bus was late this morning.

_______________

e) That's a family. The family bought our old car.

_______________

## 1 *who, which, that, whose*

Übungen ab S. 140

1. a) I know someone **who / that** can speak Chinese. b) These are the photos **which / that** Liam took on holiday. c) That's the house **which / that** I lived in when I was two. d) Jenny is the girl **who / that** sits next to me in the maths lesson. e) Some people **who / that** saw the film didn't like it. f) The tree **which / that** was in our garden fell down in the storm. g) The cakes **which / that** my aunt makes taste really good! h) The book **which / that** I'm reading is about horses.

2. a) Juliet is the girl **who** Romeo loved. b) Is Pete the boy **whose** dad is a policeman? c) The boys **whose** band is playing this evening go to my school. d) They are looking for someone **who** can help train the basketball team. e) What's the name of the actor **who** stars in that film? f) The children **whose** ball was in our garden live in our street. g) The pupils **whose** classroom is next to ours are always noisy. h) Diana is my friend **who** comes from Norwich.

## 2 Relativsätze mit Relativpronomen (*Relative clauses with relative pronouns*)

Übungen ab S. 141

1. b) Bill bought a new phone which / that was very expensive. c) The teacher asked me a question which / that was easy to answer. d) Charlotte is my friend who / that I met on holiday last year. e) Japanese is a language which / that is difficult to learn.

2. a) Football is a sport **which / that** a lot of people enjoy. b) Who is the singer **who / that** sings "Hello"? c) I've got a computer **which / that** is very slow. d) A vegetarian is a person **who / that** doesn't eat meat.

## 3 Relativsätze ohne Relativpronomen (*Contact clauses*)

Übungen ab S. 142

1. a) The people we met on holiday were really nice. b) Here's the book you wanted to read. c) I didn't see the message that was on my phone. d) They won the last match that took place on that day. e) This is the best pizza I've ever eaten! f) The hotel we stayed at was in Leeds. g) The boy who is talking to Sam is his friend. h) We live in a village that has no shops and no schools. i) Did she like the present you gave her?

2. a) I like the green jacket she's wearing today. b) The musicians we listened to played very loud music. c) The boy we saw yesterday was Frank's brother. d) The number you gave me was wrong.

## 4 Gemischte Formen (*Mixed forms*)

→ Übungen ab S. 143

1. a) Tony was the first friend ~~**that**~~ I had at my new school. b) A doctor is someone who helps sick people. c) The woman ~~**who**~~ we spoke to was very friendly. d) Fiona told me a story that was very interesting. e) A fish is an animal which lives in water. f) The flowers ~~**which**~~ I bought are for my mum. g) The man ~~**that**~~ I sat next to on the plane was from New York. h) Chocolate is something ~~**that**~~ many people like to eat. i) A baker is a person who sells bread and cakes.

2. a) Kate is the best friend I have. b) There's the dog that barks all night. c) The new vocabulary we learned was in our book. d) The bus she usually catches was late this morning. e) That's the family who/that bought our old car.

# Nebensätze (*Subordinate clauses*)

## 1 Nebensätze der Zeit (*Subordinate clauses of time*)

●○○ 1. Welches Wort fehlt in diesen Sätzen? Markiere. → Lösung S. 149

a) Mary fell asleep ____________ the end of the film.
☐ as soon as ☐ before ☐ when

b) I'll phone Jonathan ____________ I get home.
☐ when ☐ until ☐ whenever

c) ____________ Ben drinks a lot of coffee, he can't sleep well.
☐ until ☐ before ☐ whenever

d) Please be quiet ____________ everyone has finished the test.
☐ before ☐ as soon as ☐ until

e) ____________ we heard their good news, we sent them a message.
☐ whenever ☐ before ☐ as soon as

●●○ 2. Fülle die Lücken mit einer Zeitangabe. → Lösung S. 149

a) Please phone me ______________ you arrive. I'll be waiting for your call!

b) ______________ her accident, Molly couldn't go swimming for weeks.

c) I have to stay in my room ______________ I've done my homework.

d) ______________ the sun is shining, we have our sports lesson outside.

e) ______________ he was a famous actor, he didn't have any money.

f) They stayed in the stadium ______________ the end of the match.

## 2 Nebensätze des Grundes (*Subordinate clauses of reason*)

●○○ 1. Ergänze einen Nebensatz mit *because*. → Lösung S. 149

a) We're wearing scarves (wind / cold)

_______________________________________ .

b) Paul fell off his bike (road / wet)

_______________________________________ .

c) I stayed in bed (I / ill)

_______________________________________ .

●○○ 2. Schreibe Sätze aus den Wörtern und ergänze mit *because* an der richtigen Stelle im Satz. → Lösung S. 149

a) Jill / missed / bus / got up / late

Jill missed the bus because she got up late.

b) I / was / hungry / not / have / breakfast

_______________________________________

c) Claire / could / not / open / door / lost / key

_______________________________________

d) We / shut / window / cold / in the room

_______________________________________

e) Mike / got / job / needed / money

_______________________________________

## 3 Nebensätze des Vergleichs (*Subordinate clauses of comparison*)

●●○ 1. Du vergleichst im Nebensatz mit *like*.
Bringe die Wörter in die richtige Reihenfolge. → Lösung S. 149

a) like / they / it / having / are / party / sounds / a

It sounds like they are having a party.

b) she / me / like / hates / it's

c) Dad / smells / dinner / the / has / like / it / burnt

d) acts / he / my / isn't / like / friend / now / he

e) looks / going / it / like / to / it's / rain

●●○ 2. Übersetze diese Sätze ins Englische. → Lösung S. 149

a) Es ist, als ob sie uns vergessen hat.

b) Phil tut so, als ob er so klug ist.

c) Es klingt, als ob jemand ein Tor geschossen hat!

d) Es ist, als ob schon Sommer ist.

## 1 Nebensätze der Zeit (*Subordinate clauses of time*)

Übungen ab S. 146

1. a) Mary fell asleep **before** the end of the film. b) I'll phone Jonathan **when** I get home. c) **Whenever** Ben drinks a lot of coffee, he can't sleep well. d) Please be quiet **until** everyone has finished the test. e) **As soon as** we heard their good news, we sent them a message.

2. a) Please phone me **as soon as** you arrive. I'll be waiting for your call. b) **After** her accident, Molly couldn't go swimming for weeks. c) I have to stay in my room **until** I've done my homework. d) **Whenever** the sun is shining, we have our sports lesson outside. e) **Before** he was a famous actor, he didn't have any money. f) They stayed in the stadium **until** the end of the match.

## 2 Nebensätze des Grundes (*Subordinate clauses of reason*)

Übungen ab S. 147

1. a) We're wearing scarves because the wind is cold. b) Paul fell off his bike because the road was wet. c) I stayed in bed because I was ill.

2. b) I was hungry because I didn't have breakfast. c) Claire couldn't open the door because she lost her key. d) We shut the window because it was cold in the room. e) Mike got a job because he needed money.

## 3 Nebensätze des Vergleichs (*Subordinate clauses of comparison*)

Übungen ab S. 148

1. b) It's like she hates me. c) It smells like Dad has burnt the dinner. d) He acts like he isn't my friend now. e) It looks like it's going to rain.

2. a) It's like she's forgotten us. b) Phil acts like he's so clever. c) It sounds like somebody's scored a goal! d) It's like it's already summer.

# Indirekte Rede – Präsens (*Indirect speech – present tense*)

## 1 Indirekte Aussagesätze (*Indirect statements*)

●○○ 1. Überprüfe die unterstrichenen Stellen und streiche die falsche Variante durch.

→ Lösung S. 152

a) "You should practise the guitar more often."

My guitar teacher says <u>he / I</u> should practise the guitar more often.

b) "I'm very tired now."

Lucy says <u>I am / she</u> is very tired now.

c) "Sorry, we can't go with you this evening."

Paula says <u>I / they</u> can't go with <u>me / you</u> this evening.

●○○ 2. Bringe diese Sätze in die indirekte Rede.

→ Lösung S. 152

a) Tanya: "I like your new jacket!"

Tanya says she likes my new jacket.

b) Angie: "We're going to have a surprise party for Sandy."

________________________________________

c) Tom: "My brother goes to your school."

________________________________________

d) Lisa: "I'll help you any time."

________________________________________

e) Mum: "You were very rude to Mrs Martin."

________________________________________

## 2 Indirekte Fragesätze (*Indirect questions*)

●○○ 1. Welcher Satz gibt die Frage richtig wieder? → Lösung S. 152

a) "Where are you going?"
- ☐ He wants to know where am I going.
- ☐ He wants to know where I am going.

b) "Did you see Tom yesterday?"
- ☐ She asks if I saw Tom yesterday.
- ☐ She asks did I see Tom yesterday.

c) "Are you feeling better now?"
- ☐ He asks are you feeling better now.
- ☐ He asks if I am feeling better now.

d) "What does Ben want to eat?"
- ☐ She asks what Ben wants to eat.
- ☐ She asks what Ben does want to eat.

●●○ 2. Vervollständige die Sätze und berichte in der indirekten Fragestellung. → Lösung S. 152

a) "What time are we leaving?" asks Martin.

Martin asks ______________________________

b) "Are you going out with us on Friday?" Jenny wants to know.

Jenny wants to know ______________________________

c) "When is the next English test?" asks Lydia.

Lydia asks ______________________________

d) "Have you got a brother?" Simon wants to know.

Simon wants to know ______________________________

e) "What did you do at the weekend?" Chris wants to know.

Chris wants to know ______________________________

f) "Do you speak Spanish?" asks Theresa.

Theresa asks ______________________________

## 1 Indirekte Aussagesätze (*Indirect statements*)

→ Übungen ab S. 150

1. a) My guitar teacher says **I** should practise the guitar more often. b) Lucy says **she is** very tired now. c) Paula says **they** can't go with **me** this evening.

2. b) Angie says they're going to have a surprise party for Sandy. c) Tom says his brother goes to my school. d) Lisa always promises to help me any time. e) Mum says I was very rude to Mrs Martin.

## 2 Indirekte Fragesätze (*Indirect questions*)

→ Übungen ab S. 151

1. a) He wants to know where I am going. b) She asks if I saw Tom yesterday. c) He asks if I am feeling better now. d) She asks what Ben wants to eat.

2. a) Martin asks what time we are leaving. b) Jenny wants to know if I am going out with them on Friday. c) Lydia asks when the next English test is. d) Simon wants to know if I have got a brother. e) Chris wants to know what I did at the weekend. f) Theresa asks if I speak Spanish.

# TEXTVERSTÄNDNIS

# Meine Ferien (*My holidays*)

## 1 Wortschatz: Ferien (*Vocabulary: Holidays*)

●○○ 1. Finde 10 Wörter, die mit Urlaub zu tun haben. → Lösung S. 160

| | | | | | | | | | |
|---|---|---|---|---|---|---|---|---|---|
| M | O | U | N | T | A | I | N | S | T |
| W | F | T | H | U | M | O | L | Y | R |
| P | G | C | A | M | P | I | N | G | A |
| C | V | A | Q | S | D | H | Z | E | V |
| E | I | R | B | V | K | O | P | T | E |
| B | E | A | C | H | B | T | Y | S | L |
| R | W | V | A | M | R | E | L | A | X |
| Y | F | A | P | O | O | L | L | R | D |
| S | U | N | G | L | A | S | S | E | S |

●○○ 2. Welche 6 Wörter aus der Tabelle passen hier? → Lösung S. 160

a) There was a beautiful ______________ from the top of the mountain.

b) We didn't go to the beach but there was a ______________ in the hotel where we could swim.

c) If you want to save money, stay in a ______________ , not a hotel.

d) You need good shoes if you go walking in the ______________ .

e) Don't forget your ______________ ! The sun is very bright today.

f) You don't have to ______________ far to have a nice holiday – you can stay at home, too.

3. Ergänze die Wörter, die mit Wetter zu tun haben. → Lösung S. 160

a) Do you like spending your holidays somewhere ___ a ___ m?

b) Camping isn't much fun in the r___ ___ ___.

c) I hope there will be lots of ___ ___ o___ at the weekend. Then we can go skiing!

d) Allie loves it when the sun is s___ ___ n___ ___ g, but she doesn't like it if the weather is too ___ ___ t.

e) It isn't raining at the moment but it's very c___ ___ u___ y.

f) It was very ___ i___ d___ in Wales – good for sailing and flying kites on the beach!

g) You shouldn't stand under a tree during a___ to___ ___. That's very dangerous.

4. Ordne die Wörter den Themen zu.
Manche kannst du mehrmals eintragen. → Lösung S. 160

boat trip • bus • car • caravan • castle • church • climbing • cloudy • foggy • ice-skating • lake • museum • plane • pool • rainy • river • sand • sandcastle • sea • skiing • snowboarding • sunny • surfing • tent • tower • train • view • walking

Beach: ______________________________

Camping: ______________________________

Mountains: ______________________________

Sightseeing: ______________________________

Transport: ______________________________

Water: ______________________________

Weather: ______________________________

Winter holiday: ______________________________

## 2 Mein Sommerurlaub (*My summer holidays*)

1. Schreibe einen kurzen Urlaubsbericht über Felix und über Amelia. Verwende alle Informationen.

→ Lösung S. 161

a)

| | |
|---|---|
| *Name:* | Felix |
| *Where:* | Paris |
| *When:* | July |
| *What/do?* | sightseeing (Eiffel Tower) boat trip on River Seine |
| *Best thing:* | view from Eiffel Tower |
| *Worst thing:* | no pretzels to eat! |

b)

| | |
|---|---|
| *Name:* | Amelia |
| *Where:* | beach in North Germany |
| *When:* | August |
| *What/do?* | sit on beach, read magazines, listen to music, text friends |
| *Best thing:* | great ice-cream! |
| *Worst thing:* | boring with just my family |

2. Beschreibe jetzt deinen letzten Sommerurlaub.
Mache dir zuerst Notizen auf Englisch.

→ Lösung S. 161

Where did you go? ______________________________

Who did you go with? ______________________________

How did you travel? ______________________________

How long did you stay? ______________________________

Where did you stay? ______________________________

What did you do? ______________________________

What did you eat and drink? ______________________________

What was the best thing about the holiday? ______________________________

What was the worst thing about the holiday? ______________________________

## 3 Ein Telefongespräch (*A telephone call*)

1. Höre das Telefongespräch an und fülle dabei alle Lücken aus.

→ Lösung S. 162

Mrs Kent: Hello?

Ellie: Hello, Mrs Kent. It's Ellie speaking. Is Caroline there?

Mrs Kent: Oh, hello, Ellie! Yes, she's in her ______________ . I'll call her.

Caroline: Hello?

Ellie: Hi, Caroline. It's me! We're back from our ______________ now.

Caroline: Oh, hi, Ellie! I really missed you! How was your holiday?

Ellie: Well, it was … ______________ !

Caroline: What do you mean? Did you enjoy it?

Ellie: Oh, yes, we enjoyed it. But a lot of things went wrong.

Caroline: Oh no! What happened?

Ellie: Well, first we had to wait for ______________ hours at the airport because there was a problem with our ______________ . That was a bit boring, just sitting at the airport all that time. So we arrived in ______________ five hours late. And then, when we got off the plane, they told us our ______________ were not on the plane! They were lost somewhere. So we had to go to the ______________ without our bags. We couldn't even clean our teeth!

Caroline: Oh dear! Did you get your bags back?

Scanne den QR-Code und höre den Text an.

Ellie: Yes, we got them the next day, so everything was OK in the end. And Rome is a really cool city, with lots of really interesting old ______________ . My favourite was the Coliseum. When you are there, you can really imagine what it was like in Ancient Rome, when gladiators fought against lions! Anyway, I took a lot of great ______________ , and I can show you them when I see you.

Caroline: Great! Do you want to meet up tomorrow? We could go and get an ______________ .

Ellie: OK. I can meet you in the afternoon. And, speaking of ice-cream, wait till I tell you about the food in Rome! The ice-cream is amazing there, and on the last evening, I had the best pizza I've ever had in my life …

●○○ 2. Höre das Gespräch nochmal an und gib an, ob die Aussagen richtig oder falsch sind.

1

→ Lösung S. 162

| | true | false |
|---|---|---|
| a) Caroline is in the kitchen when Ellie calls. | ☐ | ☐ |
| b) Ellie had an interesting holiday. | ☐ | ☐ |
| c) Ellie didn't enjoy her holiday. | ☐ | ☐ |
| d) Ellie's family waited at the airport for four hours. | ☐ | ☐ |
| e) Ellie went to Italy for her holiday. | ☐ | ☐ |
| f) Ellie didn't clean her teeth on the first evening. | ☐ | ☐ |
| g) Ellie thinks Rome is a boring city. | ☐ | ☐ |
| h) There were lions in the Coliseum when Ellie visited. | ☐ | ☐ |
| i) Ellie is going to show Caroline some photos. | ☐ | ☐ |
| j) Ellie and Caroline are going to meet today. | ☐ | ☐ |
| k) Ellie didn't like the food in Rome. | ☐ | ☐ |

Scanne den QR-Code und höre den Text an.

## 1 Wortschatz: Ferien (*Vocabulary: Holidays*)

Übungen ab S. 154

1.

| | | | | | | | | | |
|---|---|---|---|---|---|---|---|---|---|
| **M** | **O** | **U** | **N** | **T** | **A** | **I** | **N** | **S** | **T** |
| W | F | T | H | U | M | O | L | Y | **R** |
| P | G | **C** | **A** | **M** | **P** | **I** | **N** | **G** | **A** |
| C | **V** | **A** | Q | S | D | **H** | Z | E | **V** |
| E | **I** | **R** | B | V | K | **O** | P | T | **E** |
| **B** | **E** | **A** | **C** | **H** | B | **T** | Y | S | **L** |
| R | **W** | **V** | A | M | **R** | **E** | **L** | **A** | **X** |
| Y | F | **A** | **P** | **O** | **O** | **L** | L | R | D |
| **S** | **U** | **N** | **G** | **L** | **A** | **S** | **S** | **E** | **S** |

Lösung: mountains, camping, beach, relax, pool, sunglasses, view, caravan, hotel, travel

2. a) There was a beautiful **view** from the top of the mountain. b) We didn't go to the beach but there was a **pool** in the hotel where we could swim. c) If you want to save money, stay in a **caravan**, not a hotel. d) You need good shoes if you go walking in the **mountains**. e) Don't forget your **sunglasses**! The sun is very bright today. f) You don't have to **travel** far to have a nice holiday – you can stay at home, too.

3. a) Do you like spending your holidays somewhere **warm**? b) Camping isn't much fun in the **rain**. c) I hope there will be lots of **snow** at the weekend. Then we can go skiing! d) Allie loves it when the sun is **shining**, but she doesn't like it if the weather is too **hot**. e) It isn't raining at the moment but it's very **cloudy**. f) It was very **windy** in Wales – good for sailing and flying kites on the beach! g) You shouldn't stand under a tree during a **storm**. That's very dangerous.

4.

| | |
|---|---|
| Beach: | sand, sandcastle, sea, surfing |
| Camping: | caravan, tent |
| Mountains: | climbing, skiing, snowboarding, view, walking |
| Sightseeing: | castle, church, museum, tower |
| Transport: | boat trip, bus, car, caravan, plane, train |
| Water: | lake, pool, river, sea |
| Weather: | cloudy, foggy, rainy, sunny |
| Winter holiday: | ice-skating, skiing, snowboarding |

## 2 Mein Sommerurlaub (*My summer holidays*)

→ Übungen ab S. 156

1. Musterlösung:

   a) Felix went to Paris in the summer holidays. He went there in July. He went sightseeing and visited the Eiffel Tower and the Louvre. He also took a boat trip on the River Seine. He thought the best thing about the holiday was the view from the Eiffel Tower, and the worst thing was that there were no pretzels to eat in Paris!

   b) Amelia went to the beach in North Germany for her holiday. She went there in August. She spent her holiday on the beach, where she read magazines, listened to music and texted her friends. She thought the best thing about the holiday was the great ice-cream, but she thought it was boring to just spend time with her family.

2. Musterlösung:

   Where did you go? **Ireland**
   Who did you go with? **my family**
   How did you travel? **by plane Munich-Dublin and by train to Cork**
   How long did you stay? **10 days Cork, 3 days Dublin**
   Where did you stay? **bed and breakfast**
   What did you do? **visit a few towns, beach**
   What did you eat and drink? **fish and chips**
   What was the best thing about the holiday? **people we met**
   What was the worst thing about the holiday? **cold sea water**

   Last summer I went on holiday to Ireland with my family. We flew from Munich to Dublin and then travelled by train to Cork. We stayed there for ten days, and then spent three days in Dublin before we flew back to Germany. We stayed in a small bed and breakfast in the middle of the countryside. It was very beautiful there. On some days we visited a few of the small towns nearby, and on other days we went to the beach. The water was quite cold – we always wore wetsuits! We ate a lot of fish and chips in Ireland. My dad drank Guinness, a famous black beer, but of course I didn't drink that! The best thing about the holiday was the people we met: everyone is very friendly! The worst thing was the cold sea water!

### 3 Ein Telefongespräch (*A telephone call*)

→ Übungen ab S. 158

1. Mrs Kent: Hello?
   Ellie: Hello, Mrs Kent. It's Ellie speaking. Is Caroline there?
   Mrs Kent: Oh, hello, Ellie! Yes, she's in her **room**. I'll call her.
   Caroline: Hello?
   Ellie: Hi, Caroline. It's me! We're back from our **holiday** now.
   Caroline: Oh, hi, Ellie! I really missed you! How was your holiday?
   Ellie: Well, it was .... **interesting**!
   Caroline: What do you mean? Did you enjoy it?
   Ellie: Oh, yes, we enjoyed it. But a lot of things went wrong.
   Caroline: Oh no! What happened?
   Ellie: Well, first we had to wait for **five** hours at the airport because there was a problem with our **plane**. That was a bit boring, just sitting at the airport all that time. So we arrived in **Rome** five hours late. And then, when we got off the plane, they told us our **bags** were not on the plane! They were lost somewhere. So we had to go to the **hotel** without our bags. We couldn't even clean our teeth!
   Caroline: Oh dear! Did you get your bags back?
   Ellie: Yes, we got them the next day, so everything was OK in the end. And Rome is a really cool city, with lots of really interesting old **buildings**. My favourite was the Coliseum. When you are there, you can really imagine what it was like in Ancient Rome, when gladiators fought against lions! Anyway, I took a lot of great **photos**, and I can show you them when I see you.
   Caroline: Great! Do you want to meet up tomorrow? We could go and get an **ice-cream**.
   Ellie: OK. I can meet you in the afternoon. And, speaking of ice-cream, wait till I tell you about the food in Rome! The ice-cream is amazing there, and on the last evening, I had the best pizza I've ever had in my life ...

2.

| | true | false |
|---|---|---|
| a) Caroline is in the kitchen when Ellie calls. | ☐ | ☑ |
| b) Ellie had an interesting holiday. | ☑ | ☐ |
| c) Ellie didn't enjoy her holiday. | ☐ | ☑ |
| d) Ellie's family waited at the airport for four hours. | ☐ | ☑ |
| e) Ellie went to Italy for her holiday. | ☑ | ☐ |
| f) Ellie didn't clean her teeth on the first evening. | ☑ | ☐ |
| g) Ellie thinks Rome is a boring city. | ☐ | ☑ |
| h) There were lions in the Coliseum when Ellie visited. | ☐ | ☑ |
| i) Ellie is going to show Caroline some photos. | ☑ | ☐ |
| j) Ellie and Caroline are going to meet today. | ☐ | ☑ |
| k) Ellie didn't like the food in Rome. | ☐ | ☑ |

Scanne den QR-Code und höre den Text an.

# In der Schule (*At school*)

## 1 Wortschatz: Schulfächer (*Vocabulary: School subjects*)

●○○ 1. Löse das Kreuzworträtsel und finde das Lösungswort. → Lösung S. 170

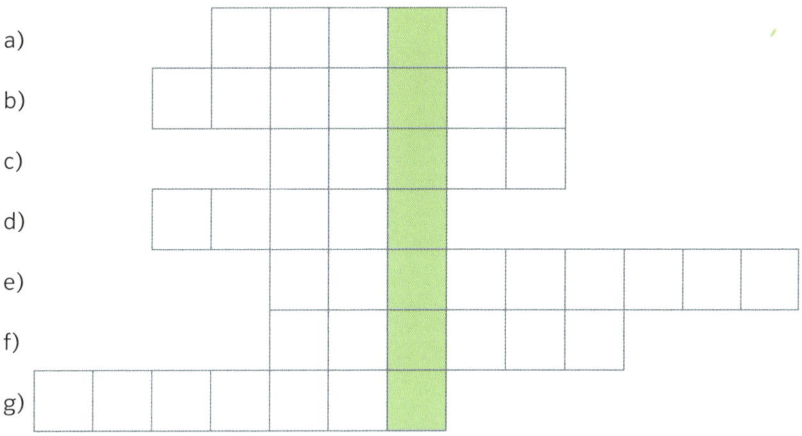


Extra word:

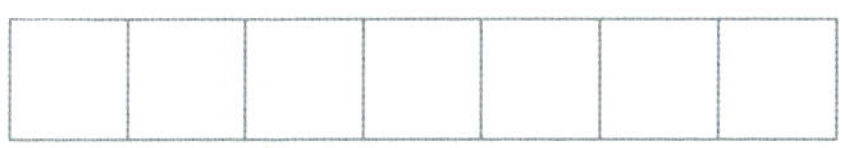

a) You have to add up numbers in this subject.

b) Learn this language and you can speak to people from London.

c) You often have to sing in this lesson.

d) You need to put on your running shoes, shorts and a T-shirt for this lesson.

e) Talk about different countries, mountains, rivers etc. in this lesson.

f) If you live in Germany or Austria, you probably speak it every day.

g) This subject teaches you about plants and animals.

●○○ 2. Ergänze diesen Auszug aus einem Stundenplan. Erkennst du alle Schulfächer?

→ Lösung S. 170

| Time | Monday | Tuesday |
|---|---|---|
| 8.00 – 8.45 | S__ie__ __e | __n__ __is__ |
| 8.45 – 9.30 | S__ie__ __e | __n__ __is__ |
| 9.30 – 9.45 | ☺ ☺ ☺ Break ☺ ☺ ☺ | |
| 9.45 – 10.30 | __ __st__r__ | A__ __ |
| 10.30 – 11.15 | __io__ __gy | __ __rm__n |
| 11.15 – 11.30 | ☺ ☺ ☺ Break ☺ ☺ ☺ | |
| 11.30 – 12.15 | __e__g__ __ph__ | __ __rm__n |
| 12.15 – 1.00 | __e__g__ __ph__ | __a__hs |

●○○ 3. Was passt nicht in die Reihe? Markiere.

→ Lösung S. 170

| | | | | |
|---|---|---|---|---|
| a) | ☐ history | ☐ geography | ☐ music | ☐ timetable |
| b) | ☐ read | ☐ jump | ☐ write | ☐ listen |
| c) | ☐ maths | ☐ English | ☐ Spanish | ☐ French |
| d) | ☐ pen | ☐ ruler | ☐ football | ☐ rubber |
| e) | ☐ drama | ☐ chemistry | ☐ biology | ☐ physics |
| f) | ☐ paint | ☐ picture | ☐ pencils | ☐ P. E. |
| g) | ☐ library | ☐ playground | ☐ computer | ☐ classroom |
| h) | ☐ teacher | ☐ mother | ☐ pupil | ☐ caretaker |

●○○ 4. Verbinde die Verben mit der richtigen Aktivität. → Lösung S. 170

| | |
|---|---|
| a) answer | a chair |
| b) spell | French |
| c) write down | a question |
| d) sit on | your homework |
| e) work with | a word |
| f) do | lunch |
| g) draw | a partner |
| h) speak | your timetable |
| i) look at | the answers |
| j) have | a picture |

●○○ 5. Füge das richtige Wort ein. → Lösung S. 170

basketball • football • run • swimming • team • volleyball • warm up

a) We play ________________ in a team of eleven people. You need to kick the ball hard!

b) In ________________ , you don't throw the ball: you hit it over a net.

c) Sometimes in P.E. we have to ________________ round and round the track.

d) It's important to ________________ before you start doing sport.

e) Anyone who wants to join the ________________ team should come to the pool at 3 o'clock this afternoon.

f) A ________________ player should be good at throwing, catching and jumping. And it helps if you are tall!

g) We play a lot of ________________ sports at school so that everyone in the class can join in.

## 2 Ein typisch britischer Schultag (*A typical British school day*)

●○○ 1. Lies den Text und versuche, den Sinn zu verstehen. → Lösung S. 171

**Ben Harris's school day**

a) My alarm rings at 7.15 in the morning. I sigh and think: "It's Monday morning again!" I slowly get out of bed and start to get ready for school. After a shower I put on my school uniform. I go to Milton Park School and all of the pupils wear a dark blue uniform. We wear dark blue trousers, a white shirt, a dark blue school jacket and a blue and yellow tie. And we have to wear black shoes or we get in trouble: no running shoes unless we're doing P. E.!

b) I always take the bus to school now that I go to Milton Park. My old school, where my younger sister goes, isn't that far from our house, but Milton Park is too far to walk. But going by bus is OK. Quite a few of my friends take same the bus, so it's nice to chat to them on the journey. And, don't tell my mum this, but sometimes I finish my homework on the bus, too!

c) We have to be in our classroom at 8.45 a.m. Our teacher calls out our names to check who is there. On Mondays and Thursdays there is assembly for the whole school. This means that all the pupils go to the gym and listen to the head teacher, who tells us some things that we need to know. We usually all sing a song together, too.

d) Our first lesson on Monday starts later, at 9.10 a.m., because of assembly. But it's a double lesson: maths. What a way to start the week! We have our first break at 10.30. If the weather is OK, we go out and kick a ball around. If it's raining, we have to stay in our classroom. That's a bit boring: we're not allowed to run around or make a lot of noise.

e) After break we have French. This is the first language I've learned and I quite like it. Today we are talking about shops and things you can buy. The lesson after French is geography. We're learning about Scotland at the moment.

f) At 12.30 it's time for lunch. Our school's got a big canteen, so we usually don't have to wait too long for our food. I'm having lasagne today. When we've finished lunch, there's time to go outside again. There are also school clubs during the lunch break. I go to badminton, but that's on Tuesday, not today.

g) The afternoon lessons start at 1.45 p.m. My class has got double history today. School ends at 3.30 and then I take the bus home. I usually have a drink and a snack when I get home, then it's time to start my homework …

●○○ 2. Welche dieser Überschriften gehört zu welchem Absatz? Eine der Überschrift brauchst du nicht. → Lösung S. 171

- ☐ Learning another language
- ☐ Clothes for the school day
- ☐ Let's eat!
- ☐ Fun at the badminton club
- ☐ The end of the day
- ☐ Take a break
- ☐ Before the first lesson
- ☐ My journey to school

●○○ 3. Lies den Text noch einmal und beantworte die Fragen. → Lösung S. 171

a) What does Ben wear at school?

b) Can he wear brown shoes to school?

c) Is his school near his house?

d) Why does the first lesson start late on Monday?

e) Does Ben like learning French?

f) Which country is Ben's class learning about in geography?

g) What is there for lunch today?

h) What can the pupils do in their lunch break?

i) What time does the school day finish?

## 3 Unsere Aufführung (*Our stage performance*)

1. Höre den Podcast genau an und markiere die richtigen Antworten.

→ Lösung S. 171

a) The stage performance at Milton Park School was ________ .

☐ last week ☐ last month

b) All the classes at Milton Park are trying to raise ________ for charity.

☐ cookies ☐ money

c) One class did a ________ to raise money.

☐ bike ride ☐ night ride

d) Class ________ put on a talent show.

☐ 9a ☐ 7b

e) Paul plays the ________ in "The Happy Cowboys".

☐ guitar ☐ drums

f) There were 8 girls in the ________ group.

☐ dance ☐ singing

g) The teachers ________ at the comedy sketch.

☐ laughed ☐ didn't laugh

h) At the end of the show, the whole class ________ .

☐ performed a dance ☐ sang two songs

i) The class made ________ money for charity.

☐ a lot of ☐ only a little

Scanne den QR-Code und höre den Text an.

## 1 Wortschatz: Schulfächer (*Vocabulary: School subjects*)

→ Übungen ab S. 163

1. a) M A T **H** S
   b) E N G L **I** S H
   c) M U **S** I C
   d) S P O R **T**
   e) G E **O** G R A P H Y
   f) G E **R** M A N
   g) B I O L O G **Y**

   Extra word: H I S T O R Y

2.

| Time | Monday | Tuesday |
|---|---|---|
| 8.00 – 8.45 | Science | English |
| 8.45 – 9.30 | Science | English |
| 9.30 – 9.45 | ☺ ☺ ☺ Break ☺ ☺ ☺ | |
| 9.45 – 10.30 | History | Art |
| 10.30 – 11.15 | Biology | German |
| 11.15 – 11.30 | ☺ ☺ ☺ Break ☺ ☺ ☺ | |
| 11.30 – 12.15 | Geography | German |
| 12.15 – 1.00 | Geography | Maths |

3. a) timetable b) jump c) maths d) football e) drama f) P. E. g) computer h) mother

4. a) answer a question b) spell a word c) write down the answers d) sit on a chair e) work with a partner f) do your homework g) draw a picture h) speak French i) look at your timetable j) have lunch

5. a) We play **football** in a team of eleven people. You need to kick the ball hard! b) In **volleyball**, you don't throw the ball. You hit it over a net. c) Sometimes in P. E. we have to run round and round the track. d) It's important to **warm up** before you start doing sport. e) Anyone who wants to join the **swimming** team should come to the pool at 3 o'clock this afternoon. f) A **basketball** player should be good at throwing, catching and jumping. And it helps if you are tall! g) We play a lot of **team** sports at school so that everyone in the class can join in.

## 2 Ein typisch britischer Schultag (*A typical British school day*)

→ Übungen ab S. 166

2. a) Clothes for the school day b) My journey to school c) Before the first lesson d) Take a break e) Learning another language f) Let's eat! g) The end of the day

3. a) Ben wears dark blue trousers, a white shirt, a dark blue school jacket and a blue and yellow tie. b) No, he can't. He has to wear black shoes. c) No, it isn't. d) The first lesson starts late because there is assembly on Monday. e) Yes, he does. f) Ben's class is learning about Scotland in geography. g) There is lasagne for lunch today. h) The pupils can play outside or go to a school club in the lunch break. i) The school day finishes at 3.30 p.m.

## 3 Unsere Aufführung (*Our stage performance*)

→ Übungen ab S. 169

2

1. Tapescript:

   Hi everyone and welcome to the Milton Park School podcast. This month I want to tell you about the great stage performance at the school last week. As you know, every class in the school has to think of a way to raise money for charity. And there have been some great ideas, from cookie sales to a sponsored bike ride by Class 9a. But the most exciting idea so far has been Class 7b's talent show.

   The show took place last Friday evening in the school hall. There was a big audience – I think all the friends and families of the 7b pupils were there! And what a show! There really is a lot of talent in that class!

   First on stage was a band called "The Happy Cowboys". This was Paul on drums, Ryan and Tommy on guitar and Chris, who sang the songs. They played some great songs, and soon the audience was clapping and singing with them.

   Next came a dance group. Eight girls performed two great dance routines. We could see that they practised very hard: their movements were perfect.

   The next act was a comedy sketch called "The Milton Park teachers' secret room." The kids dressed up as some of our Milton Park teachers and told a lot of jokes that you will understand if you are a pupil here! Everybody really laughed, even the teachers!

Scanne den QR-Code und höre den Text an.

At the end of the show, the whole class came on stage and sang two famous charity songs: "We are the world" and "Do they know it's Christmas?" Once again, the audience sang with them.

After the show their class teacher, Mrs Bennett, told me: "I am really proud of every pupil in the class! They have worked very hard on this show and organised everything themselves, even the posters! The audience had a great time and, best of all, the class made nearly £100, which is fantastic. So well done, everyone!"

Lösung:
a) The stage performance at Milton Park school was **last week**. b) All the classes at Milton Park are trying to raise **money** for charity. c) One class did a **bike ride** to raise money. d) Class **7b** put on a talent show. e) Paul plays the **drums** in "The Happy Cowboys." f) There were 8 girls in the **dance** group. g) The teachers **laughed** at the comedy sketch. h) At the end of the show, the whole class **sang two songs**. i) The class made **a lot of** money for charity.

# Einkaufen (*Shopping*)

## 1 Wortschatz: Einkaufen (*Vocabulary: Shopping*)

●○○ 1. Was kann man in diesen Geschäften kaufen? Manche Wörter passen zu mehr als einem Geschäft. → Lösung S. 177

apples • bananas • bread • butter • cake • cornflakes • crisps • eggs • ice-skates • jeans • magazines • milk • newspapers • pasta • pears • potatoes • skis • socks • sweets • tennis balls • tomatoes • trainers

a) baker's: ______________________________

b) clothes shop: ______________________________

c) supermarket: ______________________________

d) sports shop: ______________________________

e) newsagent's: ______________________________

●○○ 2. Welche Begriffe passen zu den verschiedenen Lebensmitteln? Ergänze die Sätze. → Lösung S. 177

bottles • grams • kilos • litre • packet • tins

a) How many ______________ of tomatoes do you need for the sauce?

b) Auntie May didn't have time to make a cake, so she just opened a ______________ of biscuits.

c) Can you buy two ______________ of apple juice, please?

d) I need 180 ______________ of butter for this recipe.

e) Do you want this bag with 2 ______________ of potatoes or the one with 5 ______________ ?

f) Let's get another ______________ of milk for the weekend.

●○○ 3. Kannst du die Wörter entziffern, die mit Kleidung kaufen zu tun haben?

→ Lösung S. 177

a) Where can I r-**t**-y n-o these trousers?

b) The n-h-i-**c**-g-a-n-g o-**r**-m-s-o are over there.

c) I like this k-a-**j**-t-e-c but it's too small.

d) What z-e-i-**s** is this shirt?

e) Do you have this skirt in any other l-o-**c**-r-u-s-o?

f) I'm not going to buy these trainers. They're too s-p-**e**-x-v-e-n-i-e.

g) I mustn't forget to buy some more k-**s**-c-s-o when I'm in town.

●●○ 4. Ordne diese Sätze zu einem Einkaufsgespräch.

→ Lösung S. 177

a) Thanks. Can I try them on?

b) They're £ 39.99.

c) I like them, but they're too small. Have you got them in size 38?

d) Hello. Can I help you?

e) Oh, OK. Well, I'll try them on. ... They're really comfortable! How much are they?

f) You're welcome!

g) Yes, have you got these shoes in a size 37?

h) Yes, if you sit over here, you can try them on.

i) I'll just check for you. .... Sorry, we've only got size 38 in blue, not in black.

j) I think I'll buy them. Thanks for your help.

k) Let me look. Yes, here they are in a 37.

1: ______, 2: ______, 3: ______, 4: ______, 5: ______, 6: ______,

7: ______, 8: ______, 9: ______, 10: ______, 11: ______

## 2 Geld (*Money*)

1. Höre gut zu und schreibe die fehlende Preise in die Lücken. Lösung S. 177

a) A: Excuse me. How much are these jeans?

B: They're ________________ .

A: OK, thanks.

b) A: Is this CD € 16 or € 13?

B: That one's ________________ .

c) A: A glass of lemonade costs ________________ in that café!

B: Wow! That's expensive!

d) A: These packets of sweets cost ________________ each, or you can buy 2 packets for ________________ .

e) A: Mum, can I have this jacket?

B: No way! It costs ________________ !

2. Lies die Texte über Kinder und ihr Taschengeld. Lösung S. 177

a) **Samuel:** I get £ 5 pocket money a week. I don't usually spend money on small things, like magazines or stuff like that. I like to save my money for a few weeks and buy something that costs more, like a computer game. But I usually buy some sweets once or twice a week.

b) **Liam:** My phone is really important to me and I hate it when I don't have any more credit! That's why I spend most of my pocket money on top-up cards for my phone. I get quite a lot of pocket money – £ 10 a week – but my parents say I have to pay for all my phone credit myself. I use my phone all the time when I'm not at school, so there isn't much money left for anything else.

Scanne den QR-Code und höre den Text an.

c) **Gracie:** I get £ 6 pocket money every Saturday morning and I spend it on different things. Sometimes I buy a CD or a new app, sometimes make-up and sometimes a new toy for my hamster! My dad says I should save some money, too, but I usually only save about 50 p a week.

d) **Dylan:** I get £ 5 pocket money a week, but it's not really enough now that I'm 13. So I do a few jobs to get some extra money. I wash my parents' car, cut our neighbour's grass in summer and babysit for my aunt. Sometimes my dad gives me some extra money when I help him all day in the garden. At the moment I'm saving up to buy some really cool trainers, but I still need another £ 30.

●○○ 3. Um welches der Kinder aus den Texten oben geht es hier? Du kannst natürlich nochmal nachlesen. → Lösung S. 177

a) Who saves most of their pocket money every week?

______________________________

b) Who spends some pocket money on their pet?

______________________________

c) Who does extra work to get more money?

______________________________

d) Who gets the most pocket money?

______________________________

e) Who spends most of his/her pocket money every week?

______________________________

f) Who wants to buy something expensive with his/her money?

______________________________

g) Who saves just a little bit of money every week?

______________________________

## 1 Wortschatz: Einkaufen (*Vocabulary: Shopping*)

→ Übungen ab S. 173

1. a) baker's: bread, cake,
   b) clothes shop: jeans, socks
   c) supermarket: apples, bananas, bread, butter, cake, cornflakes, crisps, eggs, magazines, milk, newspapers, pasta, pears, potatoes, sweets, tomatoes
   d) sports shop: ice-skates, skis, tennis balls, trainers
   e) newsagent's: crisps, magazines, newspapers, sweets

2. a) How many **tins** of tomatoes do you need for the sauce? b) Auntie May didn't have time to make a cake, so she just opened a **packet** of biscuits. c) Can you buy two **bottles** of apple juice, please? d) I need 180 **grams** of butter for this recipe. e) Do you want this bag with 2 **kilos** of potatoes or the one with 5 **kilos**? f) Let's get another **litre** of milk for the weekend.

3. a) Where can I **try on** these trousers? b) The **changing rooms** are over there. c) I like this **jacket** but it's too small. d) What **size** is this shirt? e) Do you have this skirt in any other **colours**? f) I'm not going to buy these trainers. They're too **expensive**. g) I mustn't forget to buy some more **socks** when I'm in town.

4. 1: d, 2: g, 3: k, 4: a, 5: h, 6: c, 7: i, 8: e, 9: b, 10: j, 11: f

## 2 Geld (*Money*)

→ Übungen ab S. 175

3

1. a) A: Excuse me. How much are these jeans?
   B: They're £ 25.
   A: OK, thanks.

   b) A: Is this CD € 16 or € 13?
   B: That one's € 13.

   c) A: A glass of lemonade costs € 4.50 in that café!
   B: Wow! That's expensive!

   d) A: These packets of sweets cost 75 p each, or you can buy 2 packets for £ 1.30.

   e) A: Mum, can I have this jacket?
   B: No way! It costs £ 80!

3. a) Samuel b) Gracie c) Dylan d) Liam e) Liam f) Dylan g) Gracie

Scanne den QR-Code und höre den Text an.

# In der Stadt (*Around the town*)

## 1 Wortschatz: In der Stadt (*Vocabulary: Around the town*)

●○○ 1. Verbinde die Gebäuden mit der passenden Erklärung. → Lösung S. 181

| | |
|---|---|
| a) church | a place to watch a film |
| b) post office | a place to watch a play |
| c) hospital | a place where people go to pray |
| d) cinema | a place where you can sleep for a few nights |
| e) station | a place for boats |
| f) theatre | a place for sick people |
| g) museum | a place to send letters and buy stamps |
| h) hotel | a place where you can buy different things |
| i) harbour | a place to see lots of interesting things |
| j) market | a place to catch a train |

●○○ 2. Verwende Begriffe aus Übung 1 in diesen Sätzen. → Lösung S. 181

a) I'm going to the ______________________ because I need to send my granny's birthday present.

b) They took Olivia to ______________________ when she broke her leg.

c) We stayed in a lovely ______________________ when we went to Barcelona.

d) My cousin got married in a beautiful old ______________________ in the countryside.

e) I like going to the ______________________ and watching actors perform live on stage.

## 2 Finde den Weg zu uns (*Find the way to our house*)

●○○ 1. Emma hat eine Sprachnachricht bekommen. Höre sie genau an und ergänze die fehlenden Wörter. → Lösung S. 181

4

Hi Emma! I'm really looking forward to seeing you next ____________ !

I'm sorry I can't meet you at the ____________ station, but you're arriving at ____________ and I've got a guitar lesson until quarter past four. But don't worry – it's really easy to find our ____________ .

When you come out of the station, ____________ left. Cross the road and go along Station Road until you get to Carlo's ____________ , then turn right. Go along ____________ Street until you get to the corner of New Street, then turn ____________ again. Go past the Mayview Hotel and go ____________ until you get to the big white church on the corner. Turn right at the church and walk along Martin ____________ until you see three big trees. ____________ the trees, there's a small red house with a white door, number 47. That's our house! See you then!

●○○ 2. Höre dir die Wegbeschreibung genau an. Verbessere die Fehler, die sich hier eingeschlichen haben. → Lösung S. 181

5

a) Turn right at the old market.

______________________________________________

b) Go past the post office.

______________________________________________

c) You'll see the shop behind the station.

______________________________________________

d) The book shop is next to the supermarket and the shoe shop.

______________________________________________

Scanne den QR-Code und höre den Text an.

## 3 Einem Touristen in deiner Stadt helfen (*Helping a visitor in your town*)

●○○ 1. Du bist in der Stadt unterwegs und triffst eine Familie aus England, die Frau bittet dich um Hilfe.

→ Lösung S. 181

Woman: Excuse me, do you speak English?

You: a) ______________________ (*du bestätigst*)

Woman: Oh, that's great! Maybe you can help us! We're tourists here but we can't find some of the things on our map.

You: b) ______________________ (*du fragst, wo sie hinwollen*)

Woman: Well, we're looking for the old castle. Is it near here?

You: c) ______________________________________________

______________________________________________

(*Erkläre den Weg: diese Straße geradeaus, am Ende der Straße rechts ab. Die Burg ist neben dem Fluss.*)

Woman: Oh, thank you! And another thing: we want to get something to eat. Are there any good restaurants nearby?

You: d) ______________________________________________

(*Du sagst, dass dein Lieblingsrestaurant italienisch ist und "Old Venice" heißt*)

Woman: That sounds good! Where is the restaurant?

You: e) ______________________________________________

(*Du erklärst: an der Burg vorbei, an der Ecke gegenüber*)

Woman: Well, thank you so much for your help!

You: f) ______________________________________________

(*Du sagst: keine Ursache und wünschst einen schönen Aufenthalt in der Stadt.*)

## 1 Wortschatz: In der Stadt (*Vocabulary: Around the town*)

→ Übungen ab S. 178

1. a) church: a place where people go to pray b) post office: a place to send letters and buy stamps c) hospital: a place for sick people d) cinema: a place to watch a film e) station: a place to catch a train f) theatre: a place to watch a play g) museum: a place to see lots of interesting things h) hotel: a place where you can sleep for a few nights i) harbor: a place for boats j) market: a place where you can buy different things

2. a) I'm going to the **post office** because I need to send my granny's birthday present. b) They took Olivia to **hospital** when she broke her leg. c) We stayed in a lovely **hotel** when we went to Barcelona. d) My cousin got married in a beautiful old **church** in the countryside. e) I like going to the theatre and watching actors perform live on stage.

## 2 Finde den Weg zu uns (*Find the way to our house*)

→ Übungen ab S. 179

1. Hi Emma! I'm really looking forward to seeing you next **week**! I'm sorry I can't meet you at the **bus** station, but you're arriving at **4 o'clock** and I've got a guitar lesson until quarter past four. But don't worry – it's really easy to find our **house**. When you come out of the station, **turn** left. Cross the road and go along Station Road until you get to Carlo's **Restaurant**, then turn right. Go along **Market** Street until you get to the corner of New Street, then turn **left** again. Go past the Mayview Hotel and go **straight on** until you get to the big white church on the corner. Turn right at the church and walk along Martin **Road** until you see three big trees. **Opposite** the trees, there's a small red house with a white door, number 47. That's our house! See you then!

2. a) Turn **left** at the old market. b) Go past the **hospital**. c) You'll see the shop **in front of** the station. d) The book shop is **between** the supermarket and the shoe shop. e) The school is **on the corner of** Hill Street.

## 3 Einem Touristen in deiner Stadt helfen (*Helping a visitor in your town*)

→ Übungen ab S. 180

1. Musterlösung:
   a) Yes, I do. b) Where do you want to go? c) Yes, it is. You have to go straight along this road and turn right at the end of the street. The castle is next to the river. c) Oh, yes! My favourite one is an Italian restaurant called "Old Venice". d) Go past the castle. The restaurant is on the opposite corner. e) You're welcome. Enjoy the rest of your stay in the town!

Scanne den QR-Code und höre den Text an.

# Im Restaurant (*In a restaurant*)

## 1 Wortschatz: Essen (*Vocabulary: Food*)

●○○ 1. Finde 10 Obst- und Gemüsesorten in dem Wortgitter. → Lösung S. 187

| | | | | | | | | | |
|---|---|---|---|---|---|---|---|---|---|
| M | B | O | R | A | N | G | E | P | M |
| N | A | P | P | L | E | W | Z | V | E |
| V | N | Y | E | W | P | K | F | D | L |
| C | A | X | A | P | O | T | A | T | O |
| S | N | S | R | D | O | N | I | O | N |
| A | A | U | P | O | L | B | R | F | J |
| S | T | R | A | W | B | E | R | R | Y |
| Q | R | T | C | A | R | R | O | T | K |
| E | L | E | T | T | U | C | E | P | I |

●○○ 2. Schreibe das richtige Wort in die Lücken. → Lösung S. 187

chicken • chocolate • pasta • rice • salad • vegetables

a) In some Asian countries people eat ______________ every day.

b) I like all kinds of ______________ , but spaghetti is my favourite.

c) I've got lettuce, tomatoes and carrots. I'm going to make a ______________ .

d) ______________ are very good for you. You should eat them every day.

e) When we go to an Indian restaurant, I usually order ______________ curry.

f) Joe's mum always bakes him a ______________ cake for his birthday.

●○○ 3. Verbinde die zwei Satzhälften, die am besten zusammenpassen.

→ Lösung S. 187

| | |
|---|---|
| a) Matt always drinks a glass of | chocolates for her birthday. |
| b) A packet of crisps is not | we gave her a basket of fruit. |
| c) Jack puts two spoons of | with a big cup of coffee. |
| d) Let's buy Anna a box of | milk before he goes to bed. |
| e) Mum put a plate of | apple cake? |
| f) When Grandma was in hospital, | a healthy breakfast! |
| g) We opened a tin of tomato | lemonade for the party. |
| h) Dad usually starts the day | sugar in his tea. |
| i) Would you like a piece of | soup: we were too lazy to cook! |
| j) We bought some bottles of | sandwiches on the table for lunch. |

●○○ 4. Jeder Satz enthält einen Rechtschreibfehler. Schreibe den ganzen Satz neu.

→ Lösung S. 187

a) Auntie Clara opened a paket of biscuits for us to eat with our milk.

______________________________

b) We had chicken and potatos for lunch.

______________________________

c) I can show you how to make French onion soop – it's really easy!

______________________________

d) They weren't very hungry, so they just had a snake.

______________________________

e) Would you like some sheese on your spaghetti?

______________________________

## 2 Im Restaurant bestellen (*Ordering a meal in a restaurant*)

1. Ergänze diesen Dialog, der in einem Restaurant stattfindet.

→ Lösung S. 188

dressing • drink • grilled • have • ketchup • order • salad • soup

Waiter: Good evening. Are you ready to ________________ ?

Luke: Yes, I think so. What is your ________________ of the day?

Waiter: Today we have vegetable or Thai chicken.

Luke: Er, I'll ________________ the Thai chicken, please.

Waiter: One Thai chicken soup. Would you like anything else?

Luke: Yes, I'd like the ________________ hamburger, chips and green ________________ with yogurt ________________ , please.

Waiter: Would you like ________________ with your chips?

Luke: Oh, yes please!

Waiter: Anything to ________________ ?

Luke: A diet cola, please.

2. Du musst auf einer Speisekarte in einer fremden Sprache nicht alles verstehen. Oft kannst du erraten, was gemeint ist. Finde Wörter in Übung 1, die zu diesen Definitionen passen.

→ Lösung S. 188

a) ________________ : a sauce that you put on a salad

b) ________________ : a way of cooking meat or vegetables

c) to ________________ : to say what you would like to eat and drink in a restaurant

d) ________________ ________________ ________________ : a special soup or other dish on the menu on that day

●●○ 3. Welche Formulierung würdest du in diesen Situationen verwenden? Kreuze die beste Lösung an.

→ Lösung S. 188

a) You're in a restaurant and want to choose your food.

- ☐ Hello? Can I have a menu?
- ☐ Excuse me, could you bring me a menu, please?

b) You want to order something to eat.

- ☐ I'd like the ham and pineapple pizza, please.
- ☐ Give me the ham and pineapple pizza.

c) The waiter brings you the wrong food.

- ☐ Hey! I didn't order this!
- ☐ I'm sorry, but I ordered the pasta, not the fish.

d) You're not sure what is in one of the dishes on the menu.

- ☐ Can you please explain what is in the "Vegetarian Surprise"?
- ☐ What on earth is a "Vegetarian Surprise"?

e) You've finished your meal and you're ready to pay.

- ☐ You can get our bill now.
- ☐ Could we have the bill, please?

4. Du bist in England und gehst in ein Café, um etwas zu essen. Ergänze den Dialog mit der Bedienung. → Lösung S. 188

Waitress: Hello! What can I get you?

You: ______________________________

(*Du möchtest die Speisekarte haben*)

Waitress: Here you are! Would you like something to drink?

You: ______________________________

(*Du möchtest einen Apfelsaft*)

Waitress: One apple juice. And to eat?

You: ______________________________

(*Du entscheidest dich für die Ofenkartoffel*)

[5 minutes later]

Waitress: One apple juice and one baked potato.

You: ______________________________ (*Du bedankst dich*)

[5 minutes later]

Waitress: Is everything OK with your meal?

You: ______________________________ (*Du bedankst dich nochmal*)

[15 minutes later]

Waitress: Let me take your plate. Would you like anything else?

You: ______________________________

(*Nein. Du möchtest aber zahlen*)

Waitress: OK. Here's your bill. That's £5.55, please.

You: ______________________________ (*Du zahlst und bedankst dich nochmal*)

Waitress: You're welcome! Have a nice day!

## 1 Wortschatz: Essen (*Vocabulary: Food*)

→ Übungen ab S. 182

1.

| | | | | | | | | | |
|---|---|---|---|---|---|---|---|---|---|
| M | **B** | **O** | **R** | **A** | **N** | **G** | **E** | P | **M** |
| N | **A** | **P** | **P** | **L** | **E** | W | Z | V | **E** |
| V | **N** | Y | **E** | W | P | K | F | D | **L** |
| C | **A** | X | **A** | **P** | **O** | **T** | **A** | **T** | **O** |
| S | **N** | S | **R** | D | **O** | **N** | **I** | **O** | **N** |
| A | **A** | U | P | O | L | B | R | F | J |
| **S** | **T** | **R** | **A** | **W** | **B** | **E** | **R** | **R** | **Y** |
| Q | R | T | **C** | **A** | **R** | **R** | **O** | **T** | K |
| E | **L** | **E** | **T** | **T** | **U** | **C** | **E** | P | I |

2. a) In some Asian countries people eat **rice** every day. b) I like all kinds of **pasta**, but spaghetti is my favourite. c) I've got lettuce, tomatoes and carrots. I'm going to make a **salad**. d) **Vegetables** are very good for you. You should eat them every day. e) When we go to an Indian restaurant, I usually order **chicken** curry. f) Joe's mum always bakes him a **chocolate** cake for his birthday.

3. a) Matt always drinks a glass of milk before he goes to bed. b) A packet of crisps is not a healthy breakfast! c) Jack puts two spoons of sugar in his tea. d) Let's buy Anna a box of chocolates for her birthday. e) Mum put a plate of sandwiches on the table for lunch. f) When Grandma was in hospital, we gave her a basket of fruit. g) We opened a tin of tomato soup: we were too lazy to cook! h) Dad usually starts the day with a big cup of coffee. i) Would you like a piece of apple cake? j) We bought some bottles of lemonade for the party.

4. a) Auntie Clara opened a **packet** of biscuits for us to eat with our milk. b) We had chicken and **potatoes** for lunch. c) I can show you how to make French onion **soup** – it's really easy! d) They weren't hungry, so they just had a **snack**. e) Would you like some **cheese** on your spaghetti?

## 2 Im Restaurant bestellen (*Ordering a meal in a restaurant*)

Übungen ab S. 184

1. Waiter: Good evening. Are you ready to **order**?
   Luke: Yes, I think so. What is your **soup** of the day?
   Waiter: Today we have vegetable or Thai chicken.
   Luke: Er, I'll **have** the Thai chicken, please.
   Waiter: One Thai chicken soup. Would you like anything else?
   Luke: I'd like the **grilled** hamburger, chips and green **salad** with yogurt **dressing** please.
   Waiter: Would you like **ketchup** with your chips?
   Luke: Oh, yes please!
   Waiter: Anything to **drink**?
   Luke: A diet cola, please.

2. a) dressing b) grilled c) order d) of the day

3. a) Excuse me, could you bring me a menu, please? b) I'd like the ham and pineapple pizza, please. c) I'm sorry, but I ordered the pasta, not the fish. d) Can you please explain what is in the "Vegetarian Surprise"? e) Could we have the bill, please?

4. Musterlösung:

   Waitress: Hello! What can I get you?
   You: **Can I see / have the menu, please?**
   Waitress: Here you are! Would you like something to drink?
   You: **Yes, I'd like an apple juice, please.**
   Waitress: One apple juice. And to eat?
   You: **I'd like / I'll have the baked potato, please.**
   [5 minutes later]
   Waitress: One apple juice and one baked potato.
   You: **Thank you.**
   [5 minutes later]
   Waitress: Is everything OK with your meal?
   You: **Yes, everything is fine. Thank you.**
   [15 minutes later]
   Waitress: Let me take your plate. Would you like anything else?
   You: **No, thank you. Can I have the bill, please?**
   Waitress: OK. Here's your bill. That's £ 5.55, please.
   You: **Here you are. Thank you again.**
   Waitress: You're welcome! Have a nice day!

# Körper und Gesundheit (*The body and health*)

## 1 Wortschatz: Körperteile (*Vocabulary: Parts of the body*)

1. Wie heißen diese Körperteile auf Englisch? → Lösung S. 194

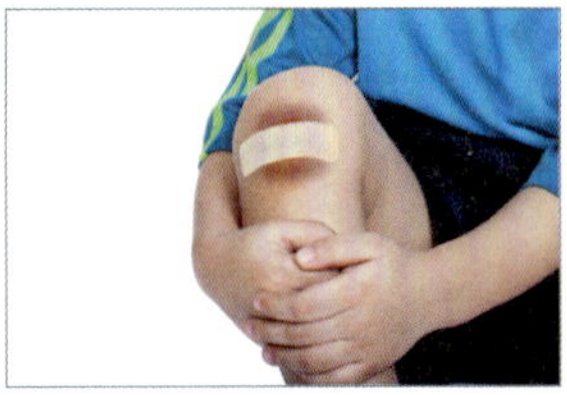

a) ____________________

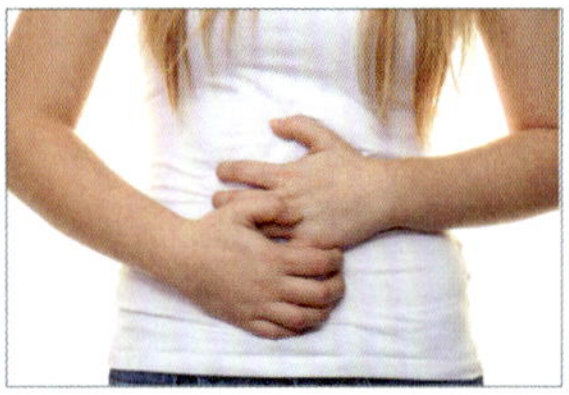

b) ____________________

c) ____________________

d) ____________________

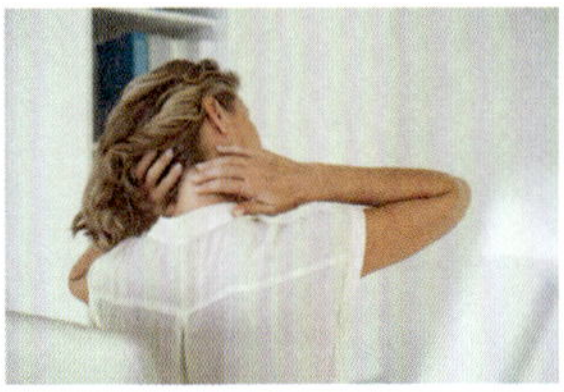

e) ____________________

f) ____________________

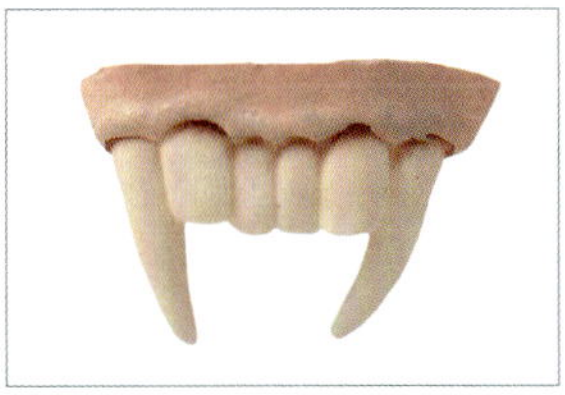

g) ____________________

h) ____________________

●○○ 2. Ergänze die fehlenden Buchstaben. → Lösung S. 194

a) Marie is wearing a hat that covers her e___ ___s.

b) My ___os___ tells me that something in the kitchen is burning!

c) Clean your ___ee___ ___ before you go to bed!

d) Tony put a warm scarf around his n___c___.

e) Please cover your ___o___th if you have to cough.

f) The bird flew down from the tree and sat on his sh___ ___l___ ___r.

g) Her ___in___ ___rs moved quickly across the piano keyboard.

h) The cat had beautiful green ___y___s.

i) The first move of this dance is: move your left ___ ___ot forwards.

●○○ 3. Kreuze an, ob die Sätze richtig oder falsch sind. Wenn du es richtig gemacht hast, ergeben die Buchstaben neben den Kästchen ein Lösungswort. → Lösung S. 194

| | true | false |
|---|---|---|
| a) We hear with our eyes. | ☐ P | ☐ S |
| b) The plural of 'foot' is 'feet'. | ☐ H | ☐ A |
| c) Our tongue is in our mouth. | ☐ O | ☐ T |
| d) We wear our shoes on our knees. | ☐ M | ☐ U |
| e) The food we eat goes into our stomach. | ☐ L | ☐ E |
| f) The plural of 'tooth' is 'tooths'. | ☐ C | ☐ D |
| g) Our toes are on our arms. | ☐ L | ☐ E |
| h) We smell with our nose. | ☐ R | ☐ A |

Extra word: ___ ___ ___ ___ ___ ___ ___ ___

## 2 Wortschatz: Gesundheit (*Vocabulary: Health*)

●○○ 1. Fülle die Lücken mit dem richtigen Wort. → Lösung S. 194

back • broke • cut • dentist's • doctor • headache • prescription • sick

a) Be quiet! All that noise is giving me a ________________ !

b) Tom ________________ his arm when he fell off a wall.

c) To help keep your teeth healthy, go to the ________________ twice a year for a check-up.

d) Catherine mustn't lift these heavy boxes because she's hurt her ________________ .

e) The doctor gave me a ________________ for some tablets.

f) Ouch! I've just ________________ my finger on this knife!

g) The ________________ told her to stay in bed for a few days.

h) Jamie ate three big ice-creams and now he feels ________________ .

●●○ 2. Bring die Wörter in die richtige Reihenfolge und schreibe den ganzen Satz auf. Man hört solche Sätze oft beim Arzt. → Lösung S. 194

a) you / how / feel / do?

________________________________________

b) got / a / temperature / have / high / you

________________________________________

c) arm / does / your / hurt / where?

________________________________________

d) to / am / examine / you / going / now / I

________________________________________

e) these / a / take / day / tablets / twice

________________________________________

## 3 Beim Arzt (*At the doctor's*)

1. Welche Übersetzung ist hier richtig? → Lösung S. 194

a) Ich muss dich untersuchen.

☐ I need to look after you. ☐ I need to examine you.

b) Ist dir schlecht?

☐ Do you feel sick? ☐ Are you bad?

c) Er hat Fieber.

☐ He's got a high temperature. ☐ He's got fever.

d) Nimm diese Tabletten.

☐ Eat these tablets. ☐ Take these tablets.

e) Sie hat sich am Kopf wehgetan.

☐ She has hurt on the head. ☐ She's hurt her head.

2. Ein Freund aus England, Luke, ist bei deiner Familie zu Besuch. Bei einem Ausflug hat er sich verletzt und muss zum Arzt. Weil er wenig Deutsch spricht, gehst du mit. Denke daran, dass du nicht alles wörtlich übersetzen musst, sondern nur den Sinn wiedergibst. → Lösung S. 194

Doctor: Hallo! Was kann ich für dich tun?

Luke: Please tell him I've hurt my foot.

You: Mein Freund a) ______________________________

Doctor: Hmm, und wie ist das passiert?

You: He wants to know b) ______________________________

Luke: You remember I went out on your bike yesterday while you were doing your homework? Well, I rode over a stone and fell off the bike!

You: c) ______________________________

Doctor: Ich verstehe. Und wo genau tut es weh?

You: d) ______________________________

Luke: It hurts here, next to my big toe.

You: e) ______________________________

Doctor: OK, lass mich sehen. Kannst du deine Zehen bewegen?

You: f) ______________________________

Luke: Yes, I can try. Ouch!

Doctor: Ja, das scheint etwas schmerzhaft zu sein. Kannst du bitte zur Tür laufen und zurück?

You: g) ______________________________

Luke: OK.

Doctor: Tut es weh, wenn du läufst?

You: h) ______________________________

Luke: Yes, a bit, but not too much.

You: i) ______________________________

Doctor: OK. Der Zeh ist nicht gebrochen. Du solltest in den nächsten paar Tagen nicht zu viel zu laufen. Ich gebe dir auch ein Rezept für Tabletten. Die nimmst du zweimal am Tag, dann wird der Fuß nicht mehr weh tun.

You: j) ______________________________

______________________________

Luke: OK, thanks. I guess that means we can sit on the sofa and play computer games all day!

## 1 Wortschatz: Körperteile (*Vocabulary: Parts of the body*)

Übungen ab S. 189

1. a) knee b) stomach c) back d) toes e) neck f) legs g) teeth h) eyes

2. a) Marie is wearing a hat that covers her **ears**. b) My **nose** tells me that something in the kitchen is burning! c) Clean your **teeth** before you go to bed! d) Tony put a warm scarf around his **neck**. e) Please cover your **mouth** if you have to cough. f) The bird flew down from the tree and sat on his **shoulder**. g) Her **fingers** moved quickly across the piano keyboard. h) The cat had beautiful green **eyes**. i) The first move of this dance is: move your left **foot** forwards.

3. a) ☐ P ☑ S, b) ☑ H ☐ A, c) ☑ O ☐ T, d) ☐ M ☑ U, e) ☑ L ☐ E, f) ☐ C ☑ D, g) ☐ L ☑ E, h) ☑ R ☐ A

   Extra word: SHOULDER

## 2 Wortschatz: Gesundheit (*Vocabulary: Health*)

Übungen ab S. 191

1. a) Be quiet! All that noise is giving me a **headache**! b) Tom **broke** his arm when he fell off a wall. c) To help keep your teeth healthy, go to the **dentist's** twice a year for a check-up. d) Catherine mustn't lift these heavy boxes because she's hurt her **back**. e) The doctor gave me a **prescription** for some tablets. f) Ouch! I've just **cut** my finger on this knife! g) The **doctor** told her to stay in bed for a few days. h) Jamie ate three big ice-creams and now he feels **sick**.

2. a) How do you feel? b) You have got a high temperature. c) Where does your arm hurt? d) I am going to examine you now. e) Take these tablets twice a day.

## 3 Beim Arzt (*At the doctor's*)

Übungen ab S. 192

1. a) I need to examine you. b) Do you feel sick? c) He's got a high temperature. d) Take these tablets. e) She's hurt her head.

2. Musterlösung:
   a) Mein Freund hat sich am Fuß wehgetan. b) how it happened / what happened. c) Er ist vom Fahrrad gefallen. d) Where does it hurt exactly? e) Es tut ihm weh neben dem großen Zeh. f) Can you move your toes? g) Please walk to the door and back. h) Does it hurt when you walk? i) Ja, es tut ein bißchen weh, aber nicht viel. j) Your toe isn't broken but you shouldn't walk too much in the next few days. The doctor is going to give you a prescription for tablets. You have to take them twice a day. Then your foot won't hurt any more.

# Tiere (*Animals*)

## 1 Wortschatz: Tiere (*Vocabulary: Animals*)

●○○ 1. Welche Erklärung passt zu dem Tier? → Lösung S. 198

a) A squirrel is
- ☐ an animal with a big bushy tail that lives in trees and eats nuts.
- ☐ a small animal that lives in a hole in the ground and eats leaves.

b) A frog is
- ☐ a kind of fish that eats insects.
- ☐ an animal that lives near water and can jump high.

c) A hedgehog is
- ☐ a small animal that looks like a mouse and lives in old buildings.
- ☐ an animal with sharp spikes on its back that lives in gardens.

d) A rabbit is
- ☐ an animal with long ears and a small round tail.
- ☐ a small animal that lives in a nest in a tree.

●○○ 2. Ordne die Tiere in die Tabelle ein. → Lösung S. 198

bird • cat • dog • goldfish • hamster • hedgehog • mole •
mouse • owl • rabbit • squirrel • woodpecker

| pets | live in trees | wild animals in the city |
|---|---|---|
| | | |
| | | |
| | | |
| | | |

## 2 Ein Tag im Zoo (*A day at the zoo*)

1. Was kannst du im Bristol Zoo alles machen?
Lies und beantworte die Fragen.

→ Lösung S. 198

**BRISTOL ZOO**
**A GREAT DAY OUT FOR ALL THE FAMILY!**

Enjoy a great day out here at Bristol Zoo! You'll love watching all our different animals as you walk around. We have lots of surprises for you, like our very special red pandas. And we have lots of other activities that will make your visit even more special!

**Daily talks and feeds**
Find out more about our animals and watch them have a meal!

✹ 11 a.m. – lions ✹ 2.10 p.m. – meerkats ✹ 3 p.m. – penguins

**Animal Meet & Greets**
For a special price, you can get even closer to some of our animals. Go behind the scenes with a keeper and come face to face with the animals!

**Zooropia walkway**
An amazing way to see the zoo! Walk across special bridges and walkways 5 metres above the ground and see some of our animals from a very different perspective! Visit our website for more information.

a) Name one of the special animals you can see at Bristol Zoo.

______________________________

b) When can you find out more about penguins?

______________________________

c) What can you do on an "Animal Meet & Greet"?

______________________________

d) How high are the special "Zooropia" walkways?

______________________________

2. Jetzt schreibst du über deinen Zoobesuch, du kannst dir etwas ausdenken. Verwende die Notizen und schreibe deinen Text.

→ Lösung S. 198

Name of zoo Augsburg Zoo

When did you visit? last weekend

Which animals did you like best? seals

Did you see zookeepers feeding the animals? yes

What was the most unusual animal you saw? rhino

What was the most dangerous animal you saw? crocodiles and snakes

Did you do any special activities? zoo quiz

What was your favourite part of the day? watching seals and giraffes

## 1 Wortschatz: Tiere (*Vocabulary: Animals*)

→ Übungen ab S. 195

1. a) A squirrel is **an animal with a big bushy tail that lives in trees and eats nuts**. b) A frog is **an animal that lives near water and can jump high**. c) A hedgehog is **an animal with sharp spikes on its back that lives in gardens**. d) A rabbit is **an animal with long ears and a small round tail**.

2.

| pets | live in trees | wild animals in the city |
|---|---|---|
| cat | bird | hedgehog |
| dog | owl | mole |
| goldfish | squirrel | mouse |
| hamster | woodpecker | rabbit |

## 2 Ein Tag im Zoo (*A day at the zoo*)

→ Übungen ab S. 196

1. a) You can see red pandas at Bristol Zoo. b) You can find out more about penguins at 3 p.m. c) You can get close to some of the animals and go behind the scenes on an "Animal Meet & Greet". d) The "Zooropia" walkways are 5 metres high.

2. Musterlösung:

   Last weekend I went to Augsburg Zoo with my family. The zoo isn't as big as the zoos in cities like Munich, but it still has a lot of interesting things to see and is a great way to spend an afternoon. And, because it isn't too big, you can really get up close to the animals.
   My favourite animals at Augsburg Zoo are the seals. I love the way they slide into their pool and swim around. They often jump out of the water onto the wall next to all the zoo visitors. I always try to get to the seal pool at feeding time – it's great fun to watch the keeper throw fish to the seals. They're really good at catching their lunch!
   One of the most unusual animals there is the rhino. There aren't many rhinos in the wild now, and the zoo shows why we must protect them. Of course there are also some dangerous animals at Augsburg Zoo! There are crocodiles and snakes in the Reptile House.
   Last weekend you could do a zoo quiz. Someone gave us a list of questions and we had to find the answers while we were walking round the zoo. There was a box at the gate for the answers and a chance of winning a prize. I hope I win! The best part of the day was watching the seals and seeing the giraffes. When the giraffes are inside their house, you can get really close to them. I think they like having visitors, too – they always look down to see who has come to their house!

# Sport und Fitness (*Sport and fitness*)

## 1 Wortschatz: Sport (*Vocabulary: Sport*)

●○○ 1. Welches Verb passt wozu?
Manche Verben passen mehrfach.

→ Lösung S. 204

catch • join • kick • lose • pass • play in • run in • score • throw • win

a) a ball: ______________________________

b) a match: ______________________________

c) a team: ______________________________

d) a goal: ______________________________

e) a race: ______________________________

●○○ 2. Wo spielt man diese Sportarten? Markiere.

→ Lösung S. 204

a) We played a great game of tennis on the new ________ .

☐ place ☐ court

b) The football ________ was very muddy after all the rain.

☐ pitch ☐ grass

c) The cup final is going to be in the Olympic ________ .

☐ Field ☐ Stadium

d) The swimming club meets every Tuesday in the main ________ .

☐ pool ☐ hall

e) Let's take our skateboards and go to the skate ________ .

☐ hill ☐ park

●○○ 3. Fülle die Lücken mit den angegebenen Wörtern. → Lösung S. 204

aerobics • climbing • court • goal • helmet • keep fit • marathon • P. E. • racket

a) I need to take my trainers with me today. We've got ________________ after the first break.

b) Maria does ________________ twice a week at the new sports centre.

c) Are you getting a new tennis ________________ for your birthday?

d) Rock ________________ isn't dangerous if you use the right equipment.

e) Jogging is a good way to ________________, and it's free, too! All you need are good running shoes.

f) You can play volleyball on an indoor ________________ or outside on sand.

g) It's a good idea to wear a ________________ when you ride your bike.

h) We thought we were going to lose, but at the last minute Lisa scored the winning ________________!

i) My brother's dream is to run in the New York ________________. I could never run that far!

●●○ 4. Verbessere die Fehler. → Lösung S. 204

a) Who won the first goal of the match?

________________________________________________

b) The dog catched the ball with its mouth.

________________________________________________

c) Our school has got a big football place for the teams to play on.

________________________________________________

d) Are you going to run for the big race next week?

________________________________________________

## 2 Mein Fitnessmonat (*My month of fitness*)

1. Lies die Texte über die einzelnen Sportler und beantworte die Fragen.

→ Lösung S. 204

In January, our school had a challenge: one month of fitness. Everybody that took part in the challenge had to write down their plan for getting fitter and healthier. Now, at the end of the month, we asked some of the pupils how they got on.

**Chris**

Fitness challenge: join the swimming club and swim three times a week
Health challenge: stop drinking cola

**How did you get on?**

Well, I joined the swimming club at the beginning of the month and I've really enjoyed it! I don't always go three times a week, but I usually swim at least twice a week and I feel much fitter. I've also made lots of new friends at the club, so that's great. But giving up cola is more difficult! I want to stop because I read how much sugar there is in one cola, but I love it so much! So I try to only drink one or two glasses every week. That's not so bad.

a) How often does Chris go swimming?

______________________________

______________________________

b) Why does he like the swimming club?

______________________________

______________________________

c) Why does he want to stop drinking cola?

______________________________

______________________________

**Louise**
Fitness challenge: run a 5 km race
Health challenge: eat 5 pieces of fruit every day

**How did you get on?**
Before this challenge I never ran more than 1 kilometre, so it wasn't easy. Luckily, my brother likes running, too, so we ran together on 4 or 5 evenings a week. I am much faster now and feel a lot stronger. My first 5 km race is next Saturday and I'm looking forward to it! Eating more fruit is easy. I eat a big fruit salad for breakfast every morning and always have an apple or a pear in my bag as a snack.

a) Was the fitness challenge easy for Louise? Why / not?

b) Does she train alone?

c) How far is she going to run in her first race?

d) What does Louise do for her health challenge?

## 3 Meine Sportarten (*What's my sport?*)

●○○ 1. Höre zu und kreuze an, um welche Sportart es geht. → Lösung S. 204

a) ☐ jogging ☐ marathon running
b) ☐ hockey ☐ ice-skating
c) ☐ aerobics ☐ karate
d) ☐ darts ☐ bowling
e) ☐ tennis ☐ golf

●○○ 2. Höre die ersten beiden Texte noch einmal an und fülle die Lücken im Text. → Lösung S. 204

You don't need a lot of ____________________ for this sport. A pair of very good ____________________ is the most important thing, although you can wear quite expensive ____________________ too, if you want to. You can do the sport alone or in a ____________________. People normally do it outside. You need to be ____________________ and fit to do this sport, because it takes quite a long time. The ____________________ people in this sport can do it in about 2 hours, but it can take as long as 6 or 7 hours!

There are two versions of this sport. One is played on a ____________________ and one is played on ____________________. It is a team sport and, especially on ice, the players wear thick clothes and ____________________ so that they don't get hurt. Each player has a long stick and they have to hit a ball into a ____________________ (on the ice it's a special type of "ball"). The game is fast and very exciting to watch!

Scanne den QR-Code und höre den Text an.

## 1 Wortschatz: Sport (*Vocabulary: Sport*)

→ Übungen ab S. 199

1. a) a ball: catch, kick, pass, throw b) a match: lose, play in, win c) a team: join d) a goal: score e) a race: lose, run in, win

2. a) We played a great game of tennis on the new **court**. b) The football **pitch** was very muddy after all the rain. c) The cup final is going to be in the Olympic **Stadium**. d) The swimming club meets every Tuesday in the main **pool**. e) Let's take our skateboards and go to the skate **park**.

3. a) I need to take my trainers with me today. We've got **P. E.** after the first break. b) Maria does **aerobics** twice a week at the new sports centre. c) Are you getting a new tennis **racket** for your birthday? d) Rock **climbing** isn't dangerous if you use the right equipment. e) Jogging is a good way to **keep fit**, and it's free, too! All you need are good running shoes. f) You can play volleyball on an indoor **court** or outside on sand. g) It's a good idea to wear a **helmet** when you ride your bike. h) We thought we were going to lose, but at the last minute Lisa scored the winning **goal**! i) My brother's dream is to run in the New York **marathon**. I could never run that far!

4. a) Who **scored** the first goal of the match? b) The dog **caught** the ball with its mouth. c) Our school has got a big football **pitch** for the teams to play on. d) Are you going to run **in** the big race next week?

## 2 Mein Fitnessmonat (*My month of fitness*)

→ Übungen ab S. 201

1. Chris: a) Chris usually goes swimming two or three times a week. b) He likes the swimming club because he's made new friends there. c) He wants to stop drinking cola because there's too much sugar in it.
   Louise: a) No, it wasn't easy for her, because she never ran more than 1 kilometre before she started. b) No, she trains with her brother. c) She's going to run 5 kilometres. d) She eats fruit salad every morning and takes fruit with her as a snack.

## 3 Meine Sportarten (*What's my sport?*)

→ Übungen ab S. 203

6

1. a) You don't need a lot of equipment for this sport. A pair of very good shoes is the most important thing, although you can wear quite expensive clothes too, if you want to. You can do the sport alone or in a group. People normally do it outside. You need to be strong and fit to do this sport, because it takes quite a long time. The fastest people in this sport can do it in about 2 hours, but it can take as long as 6 or 7 hours!

Scanne den QR-Code und höre den Text an.

b) There are two versions of this sport. One is played on a field and one is played on ice. It is a team sport and, especially on ice, the players wear thick clothes and helmets so that they don't get hurt. Each player has a long stick and they have to hit a ball into a goal (on the ice it's a special type of "ball"). The game is fast and very exciting to watch!

c) This sport comes from Japan. It was once a way of fighting, but now people learn this sport to get fit and strong, and to control their body. The people who do this sport learn to be flexible, to kick and move their arms in different ways. You can practise the moves in a group, and then you usually work with a partner. When you do this sport, you wear white trousers and a kind of white shirt tied with a belt. You can get different coloured belts when you move to the next level of this sport. People don't wear anything on their feet to do this sport.

d) This is more a game than a sport, although some people that play it make a lot of money when they win. It is something you can play at home with your friends if you have the right equipment. You need a round board with different numbers in different places, and each player has three small arrows with a sharp point. You throw your arrows at the board and try to hit a high number. The person with the most points is the winner. It helps if you are good at maths!

e) People play this sport outside. You don't play in a team, but two or more people play against each other to see who can score the most points. You play this sport on something like a big park – you need a lot of space! You have a long stick and a small ball, and the idea is to hit the ball into a hole. Sometimes you need to hit the ball a long way, but when you are near the hole a very careful hit should be enough. There is a "mini" version of this game that is fun to play with your friends.

Lösung: a) marathon running b) hockey c) karate d) darts e) golf

7

2. You don't need a lot of **equipment** for this sport. A pair of very good **shoes** is the most important thing, although you can wear quite expensive **clothes** too, if you want to. You can do the sport alone or in a **group**. People normally do it outside. You need to be **strong** and fit to do this sport, because it takes quite a long time. The **fastest** people in this sport can do it in about 2 hours, but it can take as long as 6 or 7 hours!

There are two versions of this sport. One is played on a **field** and one is played on **ice**. It is a team sport and, especially on ice, the players wear thick clothes and **helmets** so that they don't get hurt. Each player has a long stick and they have to hit a ball into a **goal** (on the ice it's a special type of "ball"). The game is fast and very exciting to watch!

Scanne den QR-Code
und höre den Text an.

# Britische Landschaften (*The British countryside*)

## 1 Wortschatz: Auf dem Land (*Vocabulary: In the countryside*)

●○○ 1. Schreibe die Pluralform für diese Tiere auf. → Lösung S. 211

a) goose ______________ d) pony ______________

b) fox ______________ e) sheep ______________

c) deer ______________ f) wolf ______________

●○○ 2. Setze ein – alle Tiere findest du auf dem Land. → Lösung S. 211

cows • ducks • foxes • goat • pony • sheep

a) My favourite part of our holiday in Wales was when we went ______________ trekking in the countryside.

b) The farmer gets up early every day to milk his ______________ .

c) We watched the ______________ swimming on the pond.

d) It was winter, so the ______________ still had their thick woolly coats.

e) A ______________ is an animal that lives on farms, but you can also find it in the mountains. We can make cheese from its milk.

f) Farmers don't like ______________ , because they try to steal chickens.

●○○ 3. Welche Tiere könntest du hier finden? → Lösung S. 211

a) in a nest: ______________

b) in a stable: ______________

c) on a pond: ______________

d) in a field: ______________

## 2 Ein Tourist in Oxfordshire (*Being a tourist in Oxfordshire*)

●●○ 1. Lies diesen Text über ein beliebtes Reiseziel in England.

→ Lösung S. 211

**Visit Oxfordshire – there's so much to do!**
Most people know the famous city of Oxford, but what about Oxfordshire? The area around the city also has a lot for tourists to see and do – you will never be bored!

**Enjoy nature**
Oxfordshire has a lot of beautiful countryside. It isn't as wild as the moors in other parts of the country, but it is great for walking or riding a bike. There are some hills but they're not too high, so you don't need to be very fit to walk there. Or why not try pony trekking? There are many riding schools in this area that can take you on a tour of the countryside.

**Really old!**
To see something really special, visit the Uffington White Horse. This is a figure in the shape of a horse, which lies on the side of a hill. It was made in the Bronze Age, so it has been there for thousands of years!

**Pretty villages**
Oxfordshire's old villages are very popular with tourists, maybe because they can take so many nice photos there! The villages are also a good place to shop for souvenirs, or have a break in a tea shop.

**The famous city**
And let's not forget the city of Oxford itself, which has everything you need for a great day out. Visit some of the historic university buildings, and walk along by the river. Buy a sandwich from the Covered Market and take it to one of Oxford's many parks. You can relax, then go and see some more of the city's famous sights, or maybe do some shopping. And, if it's raining, there are lots of museums where you can spend a few hours.

2. Beantworte die Fragen zum Text.

→ Lösung S. 211

Oxford University

Uffington White Horse

Oxfordshire village

Covered Market

a) Is the countryside in Oxfordshire wild?

______________________________________________

b) What activities can you do in the countryside?

______________________________________________

c) How old is the Uffington White Horse?

______________________________________________

d) Why do tourists like the villages in Oxfordshire?

______________________________________________

e) Where can you buy something to eat in Oxford?

______________________________________________

f) What can you do on a rainy day in Oxford?

______________________________________________

## 3 Wales und Schottland (*Wales and Scotland*)

1. Lies diese Kurzbeschreibungen und entscheide, ob es darin um Wales oder Schottland geht. → Lösung S. 211

a) This country has a lot of lakes, called lochs. People say that a big monster lives in one of them!

☐ Wales ☐ Scotland

b) The highest mountain in this country is called Snowden. It can be found in the Snowdonia National Park, a beautiful place for walking and relaxing.

☐ Wales ☐ Scotland

c) One of the most famous castles in this country is Caerphilly Castle. It dates from medieval times and is now a museum. When you visit, you will find out a lot about life in a castle hundreds of years ago.

☐ Wales ☐ Scotland

d) On special occasions, the men in this country wear "skirts" called kilts. The colours and patterns on the kilts show you which family the person wearing them comes from.

☐ Wales ☐ Scotland

e) As well as English, people in this country speak another, very old Celtic language. The government works hard to keep this language alive, and you will see that, for example, the road signs are in English and the national language. In some parts of the country, people still speak it as their first language, although today everyone speaks English, too.

☐ Wales ☐ Scotland

f) Some people in this country play a musical instrument called the bagpipes. They are difficult to play and make a special sound!

☐ Wales ☐ Scotland

## 4 Ein Foto beschreiben (*Describing a photo*)

1. Beschreibe das Bild ausführlich und benutze dabei die angegebenen Wörter.

→ Lösung S. 211

at the top • at the bottom • in the background • in the foreground • in the middle • on the left • on the right • in front of • behind • next to

## 1 Wortschatz: Auf dem Land (*Vocabulary: In the countryside*)

→ Übungen ab S. 206

1. a) geese b) foxes c) deer d) ponies e) sheep f) wolves
2. a) My favourite part of our holiday in Wales was when we went **pony** trekking in the countryside. b) The farmer gets up early every day to milk his **cows**. c) We watched the **ducks** swimming on the pond. d) It was winter, so the **sheep** still had their thick woolly coats. e) A **goat** is an animal that lives on farms, but you can also find it in the mountains. We can make cheese from its milk. f) Farmers don't like **foxes**, because they try to steal chickens.
3. a) in a nest: birds b) in a stable: horses, ponies c) on a pond: ducks, geese d) in a field: cows, sheep, goats

## 2 Ein Tourist in Oxfordshire (*Being a tourist in Oxfordshire*)

→ Übungen ab S. 207

2. a) No, the countryside isn't very wild. b) You can walk or ride a bike, or go pony trekking. c) The Uffington White Horse is thousands of years old. d) Tourists like the villages because they can take nice photos there. e) You can buy something to eat in the Covered Market. f) You can visit a museum.

## 3 Wales und Schottland (*Wales and Scotland*)

→ Übungen ab S. 209

1. a) Scotland b) Wales c) Wales d) Scotland e) Wales f) Scotland

## 4 Ein Foto beschreiben (*Describing a photo*)

→ Übungen ab S. 210

1. Musterlösung:

   This is a picture of somewhere in the countryside. There are some green trees at the front of the picture and there are two buildings behind them on the left. They look like houses. There are more trees on the left and on the right of the buildings and a field in front of the houses. Behind the houses you can see some green grass and a few more trees. In the middle of the picture I can see some hills. They are quite high, and they almost look like small mountains. They are brown, yellow and green. You can see the sky at the top of the picture. Part of it is blue but there are also quite a lot of clouds. At the moment the sun is shining, but I think it is going to rain later.

# Feiern (*Celebrations*)

## 1 Wortschatz: Feiern (*Vocabulary: Celebrations*)

●○○ 1. Um welche Feste geht es in diesen Beschreibungen? → Lösung S. 218

birthday • Carnival • Christmas • New Year • St. Nicholas • Valentine's Day

a) ________________ is a day to tell someone that you love them.

b) My sister's going to be 16 this year, so she's having a big ________________ party.

c) People in many countries celebrate ________________ by dressing up in funny costumes.

d) ________________ is a Christian holiday where people celebrate the birth of Jesus.

e) On 6$^{th}$ December, children in Germany put out their shoes so that ________________ can bring them some sweets and nuts.

f) In China, the ________________ is a very important celebration. It takes place at the end of January or beginning of February.

●○○ 2. Verbinde die Begriffe, die zusammenpassen. → Lösung S. 218

| | |
|---|---|
| a) Easter | parade |
| b) New Year's Eve | flowers |
| c) Christmas | lantern |
| d) Carnival | eggs |
| e) St. Martin's Day | tree |
| f) Mother's Day | fireworks |

●○○ 3. Welche Aktivitäten passen zu welchem Fest? → Lösung S. 218

eat a special meal with your family • eat food made with a • lot of eggs • go to church • have a big fire • look for eggs • watch fireworks • dress up

a) Easter ______________________________

b) New Year's Eve ______________________________

c) Thanksgiving ______________________________

d) Pancake Day ______________________________

e) Halloween ______________________________

●○○ 4. Schreibe die Wörter aus den Lücken in das Wortgitter. → Lösung S. 218

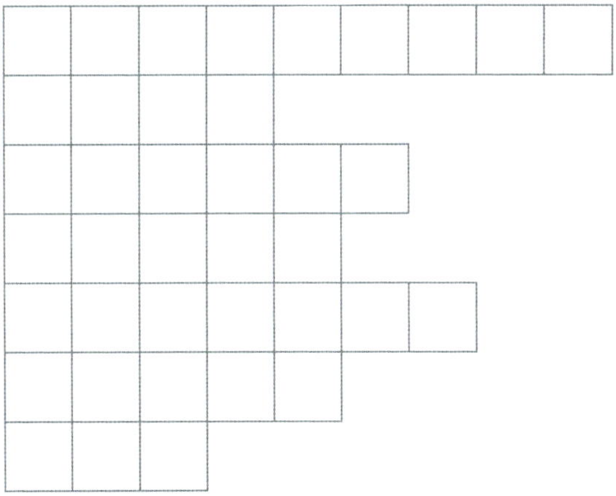

a) We're going to ______________ my grandad's 80th birthday next week.

b) Tim ______________ out all the candles on his birthday cake.

c) Let's ______________ Clare to the party.

d) Are you going to ______________ up for Halloween this year?

e) Jenny's ghost ______________ is really scary!

f) We ______________ the first candle on the first Sunday of Advent.

g) The parade was really great! Everyone had a lot of ______________ .

## 2 Wortschatz: Britisches Essen (*Vocabulary: British food*)

●○○ 1. Wie heißt dieses typische britische Essen? → Lösung S. 218

a) 

- ☐ Shepherd's pie
- ☐ Fish and chips
- ☐ Cornish pasty

b) 

- ☐ Cupcakes
- ☐ Fruit cake
- ☐ Cream tea

c) 

- ☐ English breakfast
- ☐ Scottish lunch
- ☐ Welsh dinner

●●○ 2. Vervollständige das Rezept. → Lösung S. 218

How to make Shepherd's Pie.

a) Cook some p___t___t___ ___s.

b) Fry an on___ ___n and some garlic for five minutes.

c) Add some beef and fry until the ___e___t is brown.

d) Add some vegetables, like c___r___ ___ts and peas.

e) Mash the potatoes with some milk and b___tt___ ___.

f) Put the meat and v___g___ ___ ___b___es in a dish and put the mashed potatoes on top.

g) Bake in the oven for 40 m___n___te___.

## 3 Karneval in Deutschland (*Carnival in Germany*)

1. Du bist in England und sollst für die Klasse deines Austauschschülers ein Referat über eine deutsche Tradition halten. Du möchtest über Karneval sprechen. Mache dir zuerst Notizen, dann schreibe den Text.

→ Lösung S. 219

What is the name of the celebration? ______

Who celebrates this tradition? ______

When do people celebrate it? ______

How do people celebrate? ______

Is there any special food or drink for this celebration? ______

______

Start like this:

Hi, everyone. Today I'm going to tell you about a German tradition …

______

## 4 St. Patrick's Day

●○○ 1. Lies den Text über den irischen Nationalfeiertag. → Lösung S. 219

### Saint Patrick's Day

a) Saint Patrick is the patron of Ireland. We don't really know much about St. Patrick. He was born at the end of the 4th century in Britain and probably died on 17th March, which is why we celebrate his feast day then. When he was 16, some Irish thieves kidnapped him and took him to Ireland, where he stayed for 6 years until he could go back to Britain. Later he became a priest and went back to Ireland.

b) There are many legends about St. Patrick. One is that he put his walking stick into the ground and it grew into a tree. People also believe that he used a small shamrock with 3 leaves (= Kleeblatt) to explain how God could be three persons in one. This is why many Irish people wear shamrock as a symbol on St. Patrick's Day.

c) All around the world, Irish people celebrate St. Patrick's Day. They like to show that they are proud to be Irish or that they come from an Irish family. It is important to wear something green, as this colour is a symbol of Ireland. There are also St. Patrick's Day parades, especially in cities in the USA where large numbers of Irish immigrants live. The parade in New York is the biggest in the world. Traditional Irish bands, playing pipes and drums, march in the parades.

d) You will also see other symbols of Ireland on St. Patrick's Day. One of these is a leprechaun (= Kobold), a small magical creature that wears a green suit and has a beard. Each leprechaun hides a pot of gold at the end of the rainbow. If you can find the end of a rainbow, you can have the gold. And if you catch a leprechaun, you will have three wishes for free! But be careful – a leprechaun always means trouble! There are usually people dressed as leprechauns in a St. Patrick's Day parade.

●●○ 2. Welche Überschrift passt am besten zu den einzelnen Absätzen über den St. Patricks Day in Übung 1? Nenne a) bis d). Eine der Überschriften brauchst du nicht.

→ Lösung S. 219

☐ A lucky symbol of Ireland?

☐ How to celebrate – and not just in Ireland

☐ Who was St. Patrick?

☐ Stories and symbols

☐ What St. Patrick means today

●●○ 3. Lies den Text noch einmal und verbessere die Fehler in diesen Sätzen.

→ Lösung S. 219

a) March 17th was St. Patrick's birthday.

______________________________

b) St. Patrick moved to Ireland with his parents when he was 16.

______________________________

c) St. Patrick used a tree to explain about God.

______________________________

d) You mustn't wear anything green on St. Patrick's Day.

______________________________

e) The St. Patrick's Day parade is not very important in New York.

______________________________

f) A leprechaun will always bring you good luck.

______________________________

g) St. Patrick was born in Ireland.

______________________________

## 1 Wortschatz: Feiern (*Vocabulary: Celebrations*)

→ Übungen ab S. 212

1. a) **Valentine's Day** is a day to tell someone that you love them. b) My sister's going to be 16 this year, so she's having a big **birthday** party. c) People in many countries celebrate **Carnival** by dressing up in funny costumes. d) **Christmas** is a Christian holiday where people celebrate the birth of Jesus. e) On 6th December, children in Germany put out their shoes so that **St. Nicholas** can bring them some sweets and nuts. f) In China, the **New Year** is a very important celebration. It takes place at the end of January or beginning of February.

2. a) Easter – eggs b) New Year's Eve – fireworks c) Christmas – tree d) Carnival – parade e) St. Martin's Day – lantern f) Mother's Day – flowers

3. a) Easter: **go to church**, **look for eggs** b) New Year's Eve: **watch fireworks** c) Thanksgiving: **eat a special meal with your family** d) Pancake Day: **eat food made with a lot of eggs** e) Halloween: **dress up**

4.

| | | | | | | | | |
|---|---|---|---|---|---|---|---|---|
| C | E | L | E | B | R | A | T | E |
| B | L | E | W | | | | | |
| I | N | V | I | T | E | | | |
| D | R | E | S | S | | | | |
| C | O | S | T | U | M | E | | |
| L | I | G | H | T | | | | |
| F | U | N | | | | | | |

a) celebrate b) blew c) invite d) dress e) costume f) light g) fun

## 2 Wortschatz: Britisches Essen (Vocabulary: *British food*)

→ Übungen ab S. 214

1. a) Fish and chips b) Cream tea c) English breakfast

2. a) Cook some **potatoes** until they are soft. b) Fry an **onion** and some garlic for five minutes. c) Add some beef and fry until the **meat** is brown. d) Add some vegetables, like **carrots** and peas. e) Mash the potatoes with some milk and **butter**. f) Put the meat and **vegetables** in a dish and put the mashed potatoes on top. g) Bake in the oven for 40 **minutes**.

## 3 Karneval in Deutschland (*Carnival in Germany*)

→ Übungen ab S. 215

1. Musterlösung:

What is the name of the celebration? **Karneval**
Who celebrates this tradition? **people all over Germany – biggest in Cologne**
When do people celebrate it? **Nov 11$^{th}$ until six weeks before Easter**
How do people celebrate? **costumes, parties, parade**
Is there any special food or drink for this celebration? **cake**

Hi, everyone. Today I'm going to tell you about a German tradition called Karneval. People also call it „Fasching". People celebrate „Karneval" all over Germany, but the biggest celebrations are in Cologne. It is one of the most important celebrations of the year there and it is a time to have fun.
Karneval starts on November 11$^{th}$ at 11:11 in the morning and it is celebrated until six weeks before Easter. The biggest celebrations are in the last week of Karneval, and the last day is always a Tuesday. After that, everything is quiet again.
People celebrate Karneval by dressing up in funny costumes. Children like dressing up, of course, but the adults do it, too. There are a lot of parties at this time of year, with singing, dancing and jokes. There are dancing shows and bands play. And most cities have a parade in the last weeks of Karneval. The people in the parade throw sweets for the kids who are watching.
At this time of year people eat a special kind of cake. It tastes really good! You can have a lot of fun at Karneval!

## 4 St. Patrick's Day

→ Übungen ab S. 216

2. a) Who was St. Patrick? b) Stories and symbols c) How to celebrate – and not just in Ireland d) A lucky symbol of Ireland?

3. a) March 17$^{th}$ was the day St. Patrick died. b) Some thieves kidnapped him and took him to Ireland when he was 16. c) St. Patrick used a shamrock to explain about God. d) It is traditional to wear something green on St. Patrick's Day. e) The St. Patrick's Day parade in New York is the biggest in the world. f) A leprechaun might make trouble for you. g) St. Patrick was born in Britain.

# Internet, Briefe und Smartphones (*Internet, letters and smartphones*)

## 1 Wortschatz: Schreiben (*Vocabulary: Writing*)

●○○ 1. Schreibe die fehlenden Wörter in die Lücken. → Lösung S. 222

commented • forum • profile • receive • social network • text message • video chat

a) My ______________ picture is of me and my cat.

b) Please send Mum a ______________ when you arrive.

c) Gracie didn't ______________ my e-mail.

d) She asked a question about her dog in an online ______________ .

e) We sometimes ______________ with my uncle and aunt in Australia.

f) Ten people have already ______________ on my new photo!

g) Ellie's got more than two hundred friends on that ______________ .

●○○ 2. Markiere die richtige Alternative. → Lösung S. 222

a) How often do you ________ your messages?

☐ look ☐ check

b) Tom has just ________ a new photo.

☐ made ☐ posted

c) Why didn't you ________ my text message?

☐ reply to ☐ send

d) Samuel ________ a new app for his smartphone.

☐ downloaded ☐ joined

## 2 Brief an eine Webpage (*Letter to a webpage*)

1. Du hast ein Problem mit deinen Eltern: Du willst auf eine Party gehen, aber sie erlauben es dir nicht. Du schreibst einen Brief an dein Lieblings-Online-Magazin, „Teen Chat".

→ Lösung S. 222

These notes will help you with your letter:

- Start with a greeting
- Writing – need help with a problem
- The problem is …
- Ask for advice
- Don't forget to say "thank you"
- Write you name

## 1 Wortschatz: Schreiben (*Vocabulary: Writing*)

→ Übungen ab S. 220

1. a) My **profile** picture is of me and my cat. b) Please send Mum a **text message** when you arrive. c) Gracie didn't **receive** my e-mail. d) She asked a question about her dog in an online **forum**. e) We sometimes **video chat** with my uncle and aunt in Australia. f) Ten people have already **commented** on my new photo! g) Ellie's got more than two hundred friends on that **social network**.

2. a) How often do you **check** your messages? b) Tom has just **posted** a new photo. c) Why didn't you **reply to** my text message? d) Samuel **downloaded** a new app for his smartphone.

## 2 Brief an eine Webpage (*Letter to a webpage*)

→ Übungen ab S. 221

1. Musterlösung:

   Dear Rob,
   I'm writing to you because I really need help with a problem. There's a big party at my friend's house this weekend but my parents say I can't go. It isn't fair! Nearly everyone else in my class is going! But my parents don't know my friend and they say I'm too young to go (I'm 13). How can I show my parents that everything will be OK? I really want to go to this party with all my friends! What do you think?
   Thank you for your help!
   Yours, Max

# Ein Star sein (*Being a star*)

## 1 Wortschatz: Berühmt sein (*Vocabulary: Being famous*)

●○○ 1. Wofür sind diese Menschen berühmt? → Lösung S. 226

actor • footballer • model • musician • writer

a) Gary plays for a London football club. He's a ____________________ .

b) You can see Charlotte's photo in magazines. She wears designer clothes because she's a ____________________ .

c) Tom is the star of many Hollywood films. He's an ____________________ .

d) Tina is a ____________________ . Her band had a number one hit last year.

e) J. K. Rowling is famous because of her "Harry Potter" books. She's a ____________________

●○○ 2. Ergänze die Sätze mit dem Verb in Klammern. Du benötigst hier das *present perfect*. → Lösung S. 226

a) The band ____________________ a new album. (record)

b) Steve ____________________ another silver medal. (win)

c) They ____________________ in some plays on Broadway. (act)

d) Linda ____________________ filming her new action movie. (finish)

e) Jack is a guitarist who ____________________ with some of the world's greatest rock musicians. (tour)

f) Julia ____________________ many best-selling stories for children. (write)

## 2 Notizen über einen Star (*Notes on a star*)

●○○ 1. Lies den Text über einen berühmten Schauspieler. → Lösung S. 226

a) But there is one big difference between Daniel Radcliffe and other teenagers: he is very rich! He made millions of pounds from the "Harry Potter" films, but has always said that the money was not important to him. He does not keep all the money for himself, but supports different charities for children and young people.

b) One last thing we can say about Daniel Radcliffe is that he's a nice guy. He isn't arrogant about being famous and takes time for his fans. When you see him on a talk show, he always seems very friendly, laughing and joking. And, because he's also a good actor, I think he will still be popular for many more years!

c) Daniel was only 11 years old when he got the part of the boy who finds out he's a wizard. In the first film, he didn't know it would be so popular and that he would play the role of Harry for the next 10 years. Of course, this means that he had a very different life from most teenagers. But Daniel says he didn't have a bad time because his family always helped him.

d) Do you know the name Daniel Radcliffe? If you're not sure, I can tell you that you have definitely seen a picture of him in his most famous film role. Daniel Radcliffe is the actor who played Harry Potter in all eight films in the series. With his dark hair, round glasses and magic wand, for many people Daniel is Harry Potter.

e) Since finishing the last Potter film, Daniel has looked for parts that are very different from the boy wizard. He has not acted in any more films for children, but has chosen roles in horror films and thrillers. He has also worked in the theatre and has been in plays both in England and America. He has shown that he can play very different kinds of roles and be more than "just" Harry Potter. But he is still happy if people remember him as Harry Potter.

2. Die Absätze des Artikels über Daniel Radcliffe sind durcheinandergekommen. Bringe sie wieder in die richtige Reihenfolge.

→ Lösung S. 226

1: ___ , 2: ___ , 3: ___ , 4: ___ , 5: ___

3. Lies den Text noch einmal beantworte die Fragen.

→ Lösung S. 226

a) How old was Daniel Radcliffe when he became famous?

______________________________

b) How many "Harry Potter" films did he star in?

______________________________

c) How long did he play the part of Harry?

______________________________

d) Why is Daniel different from other people of his age?

______________________________

e) What kind of films has Daniel made since "Harry Potter"?

______________________________

4. Sind diese Aussagen richtig oder falsch?

→ Lösung S. 226

| | true | false |
|---|---|---|
| a) Daniel was a typical teenager. | ☐ | ☐ |
| b) He uses his money to help other people. | ☐ | ☐ |
| c) He hates it when people remember him as Harry Potter. | ☐ | ☐ |
| d) He makes a lot of children's films now. | ☐ | ☐ |
| e) He is very arrogant. | ☐ | ☐ |
| f) He is a good actor. | ☐ | ☐ |

## 1 Wortschatz: Berühmt sein (*Vocabulary: Being famous*)

→ Übungen ab S. 223

1. a) Gary plays for a London football club. He's a **footballer**. b) You can see Charlotte's photo in magazines. She wears designer clothes because she's a **model**. c) Tom is the star in many Hollywood films. He's an **actor**. d) Tina is a **musician**. Her band had a number one hit last year. e) J. K. Rowling is famous because of her "Harry Potter" books. She's a **writer**.

2. a) The band **has recorded** a new album. b) Steve **has won** another silver medal. c) They **have acted** in some plays on Broadway. d) Linda **has finished** filming her new action movie. e) Jack is a guitarist who **has toured** with some of the world's greatest rock musicians. f) Julia **has written** many best-selling stories for children.

## 2 Notizen über einen Star (*Notes on a star*)

→ Übungen ab S. 224

2. 1: **d**; 2: **c**; 3: **a**; 4: **e**; 5: **b**

3. a) Daniel Radcliffe was 11 when he became famous. b) He starred in 8 "Harry Potter" films. c) He played the part of Harry for 10 years. d) Daniel is different because he is very rich. e) Since "Harry Potter", he's made horror films and thrillers.

4.

| | true | false |
|---|---|---|
| a) Daniel was a typical teenager. | ☐ | ☑ |
| b) He uses his money to help other people. | ☑ | ☐ |
| c) He hates it when people remember him as Harry Potter. | ☐ | ☑ |
| d) He makes a lot of children's films now. | ☐ | ☑ |
| e) He is very arrogant. | ☐ | ☑ |
| f) He is a good actor. | ☑ | ☐ |

# Ausflug in die britische Geschichte (*A trip into British history*)

## 1 Wortschatz: Britische Geschichte (*Vocabulary: British history*)

●○○ 1. Setze die Wörter in das Wortgitter ein. → Lösung S. 233

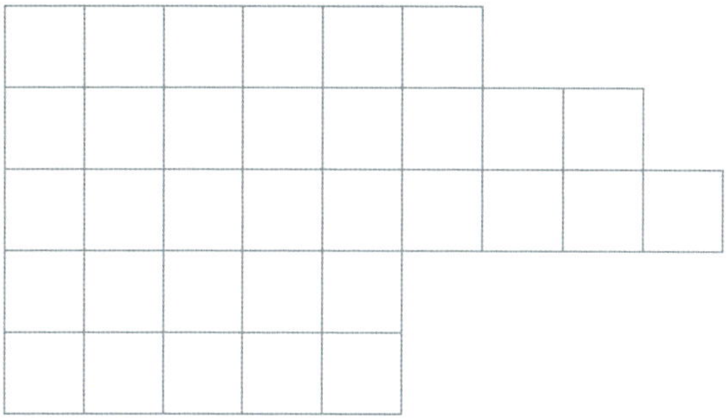

bracelets • music • tribes • warriors • Welsh

a) Celtic ______________ lived in Britain for hundreds of years before the Romans arrived.

b) The Celts were ______________ , which means they often fought each other.

c) But they also made beautiful objects, like ______________ , with special designs.

d) One of the Celtic languages that many people still speak today is ______________ .

e) Culture was important, and the Celts had their own ______________ and art.

●○○ 2. Fülle die Lücken. → Lösung S. 233

baths • chat • floors • goddess • hot • massage • slaves • spring

One of the most famous Roman sites in Britain is the Roman ______________ in the city of Bath. The Romans built them around a natural hot ________________ . This was already a special place for the Celts and their ______________ Sulis, which is why the Romans called it "Aquae Sulis", meaning "the waters of Sulis". They changed her name to Minerva and built a wonderful place for getting clean. The baths have ______________ , warm and cold rooms, rooms to relax in and rooms to sit and ______________ to friends in. Many ______________ worked there, to give the visitors a ______________ , for example. Visitors today can get a really clear idea of what a Roman bathhouse was like. They walk across the original stone ______________ and can see the original hot spring, too.

●●○ 3. Großbritannien ist ein Land voller Legenden. Kannst du die Wörter ergänzen, die zu dieser Legende passen? → Lösung S. 233

a) King Arthur was a Celtic k___ ___gh___ .

b) When they met in their castle, King Arthur and his friends sat at the R___ ___n___ T___ ___l___ .

c) Arthur had a ___wo___d called Excalibur. When he pulled it out of a___t___ne, everyone knew that he would be the next k___ ___g.

d) Arthur and the other knights often had to fight b___ ___t___es against their en___ ___i___s.

e) Excalibur had ma___ ___cal powers and helped Arthur to win.

## 2 Klassenausflug an einen historischen Ort (*A class trip to a historic place*)

1. Lies zunächst die Informationen über einen alten römischen Ort in England.

→ Lösung S. 233

St. Albans is a town just to the north of London, and was one of the biggest Roman settlements in Britain. The Roman name for the settlement was Verulamium, and you can still see some of the original parts today.

The Hypocaust dates from the 2$^{nd}$ century A.D. A hypocaust was a kind of heating system for Roman buildings. It was a way for hot air to get under the floor and through the walls. The floor is covered by a mosaic.

Verulamium also had a big Roman theatre. It is the only Roman theatre in Britain that had a stage (the Romans usually built amphitheatres, where the people looked down on the action happening in the middle of the theatre). There was room for 2,000 people in the theatre. They went there to see dancing, religious processions and, of course, fighting, including shows with wild animals. You can visit the ruins and imagine what it was like to watch a show there. School classes are welcome and pay £1 for each pupil.

If you want to find out more about the Romans in Britain, visit the Verulamium Museum. Visitors can see Roman rooms and find out how the people really lived in the settlement. The museum is great for children because of the many hands-on displays, where they can really discover a lot about Roman life.

2. Du hast mit deiner Klasse die römische Ausgrabungen bei St. Albans besucht. Jetzt musst du ein Bericht über den Ausflug schreiben. Mache dir zuerst Notizen. → Lösung S. 233

**Beginning:**

Who went on the trip? ______________________

Why did you go? ______________________

When? ______________________

Where? ______________________

How did you get there? ______________________

**Middle paragraph(s):**

What did you do and see? ______________________

Where did you have lunch? ______________________

Did anything interesting / funny / exciting / surprising happen?

______________________

______________________

______________________

**Last paragraph:**

What was the best part of the trip?

______________________

______________________

Did you enjoy it? Why or why not? Would you like to go there again?

______________________

______________________

●●○ 3. Schreibe deinen Bericht. Wenn du fertig bist, lies ihn aufmerksam durch und kontrolliere, ob du keine Fehler gemacht hast.

→ Lösung S. 234

## 3 Beschreibung einer keltischen Sehenswürdigkeit (*A description of a Celtic site*)

●●○ 1. Du wirst die Beschreibung einer keltischen Siedlung aus der Eisenzeit hören. Höre aufmerksam zu. Dann fülle die Lücken in dem Text aus.

8

→ Lösung S. 235

Hello and welcome to our audio tour of Castell Henllys, the Iron Age settlement in the heart of Pembrokeshire, Wales. The buildings are reconstructed to look exactly as they did ______________ years ago, when people lived here. As you listen, you can walk from building to building and learn a lot about ______________ in a Celtic village.

Leave the ______________ Centre and walk up the hill. You will see the ______________ on your left. People caught fish here, and we know that they also had ______________ .

Near the village gate, you can see the herb ______________ . The people who lived here used the herbs for cooking, dyeing their ______________ different colours and for medicine.

●●○ 2. Höre den zweiten Teil des Textes an und überprüfe diese Aussagen. Verbessere die Fehler.

→ Lösung S. 235

a) It was a good idea to build the village on top of a hill.

______________________________________________

b) It was not possible to cook food in the Chief's House.

______________________________________________

c) The Celts did not decorate their homes.

______________________________________________

d) The villagers often sat together and listened to stories.

______________________________________________

Scanne den QR-Code und höre den Text an.

## 1 Wortschatz: Britische Geschichte (*Vocabulary: British history*)

Übungen ab S. 227

1.

| | | | | | | | | |
|---|---|---|---|---|---|---|---|---|
| T | R | I | B | E | S | | | |
| W | A | R | R | I | O | R | S | |
| B | R | A | C | E | L | E | T | S |
| W | E | L | S | H | | | | |
| M | U | S | I | C | | | | |

2. One of the most famous Roman sites in Britain is the Roman **baths** in the city of Bath. The Romans built them around a natural hot **spring**. This was already a special place for the Celts and their **goddess** Sulis, which is why the Romans called it "Aquae Sulis", meaning "the waters of Sulis". They changed her name to Minerva and built a wonderful place for getting clean. The baths have **hot**, warm and cold rooms, rooms to relax in and rooms to sit and **chat** to friends in. Many **slaves** worked there, to give the visitors a **massage**, for example. Visitors today can get a really clear idea of what a Roman bathhouse was like. They walk across the original stone **floors** and can see the original hot spring, too.

3. a) King Arthur was a Celtic **knight**. b) When they met in their castle, King Arthur and his friends sat at the **Round Table**. c) Arthur had a **sword** called Excalibur. When he pulled it out of a **stone**, everyone knew that he would be the next **king**. d) Arthur and the other knights often had to fight **battles** against their **enemies**. e) Excalibur had **magical** powers and helped Arthur to win.

## 2 Klassenausflug an einen historischen Ort (*A class trip to a historic place*)

Übungen ab S. 229

2. Musterlösung – Notizen:
   **Beginning:**
   who: 7c why: as part of our history lesson; when: last week; where: class trip to St. Albans; how: by bus
   **Middle paragraph(s):**
   Saw the hypocaust, the Roman theatre and the museum.
   Had sandwiches for lunch
   Hypocaust: a bit boring; only nice mosaic floor; interesting: the theatre, but it started raining; something funny in the museum: we learned that Romans all went to the toilet together!
   **Last paragraph:**
   Best part: seeing how people lived in Roman Britain; worst part: rain; yes, I enjoyed it and would go again

3. Musterlösung:

   Last week my class, Class 7c, went on a trip to St. Albans. We went there because we're learning about Roman Britain in our history lessons, and there was a Roman settlement at St. Albans. It isn't very far from our school in London, so we went there by bus.

   There are different things to see in St. Albans, which was called Verulamium in Roman times. One of them is the hypocaust, which was a kind of heating system. I thought that was a bit boring, because there wasn't much to see there. But there was a really nice mosaic on the floor. Then we went to the Roman theatre. This is only a ruin now, but you can still imagine what it was like to go there and watch people fighting wild animals! We all had sandwiches with us, and we ate them outside at the theatre.

   But then it started raining, and our teacher, Mrs Murphy, said we had to go to the museum instead. The museum was very interesting, with lots of Roman objects that people found near here. You learn a lot about Roman life there. We all really laughed when we found out that Romans always went to the toilet together and had a chat while they were sitting there!

   I think the best part of the trip was learning funny facts about Roman life, and the worst part was the rain. But I liked visiting St. Albans and I would go there again.

## 3 Beschreibung einer keltischen Sehenswürdigkeit (*A description of a Celtic site*)

→ Übungen ab S. 232

8

1. Hello and welcome to our audio tour of Castell Henllys, the Iron Age settlement in the heart of Pembrokeshire, Wales. The buildings are reconstructed to look exactly as they did **2,000** years ago, when people lived here. As you listen, you can walk from building to building and learn a lot about **life** in a Celtic village.

   Leave the **Visitor** Centre and walk up the hill. You will see the **river** on your left. People caught fish here, and we know that they also had **boats**.

   Near the village gate, you can see the herb **garden**. The people who lived here used the herbs for cooking, dyeing their **clothes** different colours and for medicine.

   Now go into the village. As you can see, it is on top of a hill. This was a good idea, because the people who lived there could see if warriors from another tribe were coming to attack them. Today you can enjoy the view of the hills and countryside from here.

Scanne den QR-Code und höre den Text an.

The first big building on your right is the Chief's House. The Chief was the most important person in the tribe. There is a fire in the middle for cooking, beds and even a wall painting. The Celts liked to make their homes look attractive.

Now go and look at the building opposite the Chief's House. This is the forge, the place where they heated iron to make it into tools.

Next, you can visit the Meeting House. You can image how the whole village would come together here and sit on the wooden seats around the fire. Story-telling was very popular in Celtic times and, because there were no books, was an important way of passing on stories and legends.

We hope you have enjoyed looking round Castell Henllys! There is more information about the village in the Visitor Centre. And, if you have any questions, just ask one of our guides! They can tell you anything you want to know. Goodbye and hope to see you again!

Lösung:

1. Hello and welcome to our audio tour of Castell Henllys, the Iron Age settlement in the heart of Pembrokeshire, Wales. The buildings are reconstructed to look exactly as they did **2,000** years ago, when people lived here. As you listen, you can walk from building to building and learn a lot about **life** in a Celtic village.

   Leave the **Visitor** Centre and walk up the hill. You will see the **river** on your left. People caught fish here, and we know that they also had **boats**.

   Near the village gate, you can see the herb **garden**. The people who lived here used the herbs for cooking, dyeing their **clothes** different colours and for medicine.

2. a) True b) False. There was a fire for cooking in the Chief's House. c) False. There were wall paintings in the houses. d) True

# Reise nach England (*Trip to England*)

## 1 Wortschatz: Ankunft in England (*Vocabulary: Arrival in England*)

●○○ 1. Bringe die unterstrichene Wörter in die richtige Reihenfolge. Beginne mit dem fett gedruckten.

→ Lösung S. 238

a) Felix is a u-g-**l**-e-a-n-a-g student who is going to spend three weeks in England.

b) His family take him to the i-p-r-r-**a**-o-t to catch his plane.

c) He looks at the information o-r-d-**b**-a to find his flight.

d) He goes to the check-in desk in e-m-**T**-r-i-l-a-n 2.

e) He waits in the e-p-a-**d**-r-u-t-e-r lounge until it is time to get on the plane.

f) The flight takes two hours and soon the plane a-s-d-n-**l** in London.

g) Felix goes to the g-a-g-a-**b**-e-g hall to get his rucksack. Now he's excited about meeting his host family!

●○○ 2. Ergänze die Lücken.

→ Lösung S. 238

arrivals • ferry • left • passport • Tunnel

a) If you go to Britain by car, remember to drive on the ______________ !

b) Departures are here and ______________ are downstairs.

c) We took the ______________ from Calais to Dover. It was nice to sail across the English Channel.

d) The train journey through the Channel ______________ is very fast.

e) You have to show your ______________ when you travel to Britain.

## 2 In der Gastfamilie (*Guest in a foreign family*)

1. Du wohnst bei einer Gastfamilie in England, weil du dort einen Sprachkurs besuchst. Du willst höflich und hilfreich sein, während du bei der Familie bist. Was könntest du in diesen Situationen sagen?

→ Lösung S. 238

Welche Formulierungen kannst du hier verwenden?

- Shall I …?
- Could you … please?
- Is it OK if …?
- What shall I do with …?
- Where/How can I …?

*You want to phone your family in Germany.*

You: a) ______________________________

Host mum: Yes, of course you can! Or, if you like, you can Skype with them on the computer.

*You have finished your meal and you want to help clear the table.*

You: b) ______________________________

Host mum: Oh, thanks! You can put the dirty plates and glasses in the dishwasher.

*You have some dirty clothes.*

You c) ______________________________

Host mum: Yes. I'll show you where the washing machine is.

*You want to go out with some friends in the evening.*

You: d) ______________________________

Host mum: Yes, it's OK, but you must be back before 10 o'clock.

*You don't know where to catch the bus to the city centre.*

You: e) ______________________________

Host mum: The bus stop is at the end of the road.

## 1 Wortschatz: Ankunft in England (*Vocabulary: Arrival in England*)

→ Übungen ab S. 236

1. a) Felix is a **language** student who is going to spend three weeks in England. b His family take him to the **airport** to catch his plane. c) He looks at the information **board** to find his flight. d) He goes to the check-in desk in **Terminal** 2. e) He waits in the **departure** lounge until it is time to get on the plane. f) The flight takes two hours and soon the plane **lands** in London. g) Felix goes to the **baggage** hall to get his rucksack. Now he's excited about meeting his host family!

2. a) If you go to Britain by car, remember to drive on the **left**! b) Departures are here and **Arrivals** are downstairs. c) We took the **ferry** from Calais to Dover. It was nice to sail across the English Channel. d) The train journey through the Channel **Tunnel** is very fast. e) You have to show your **passport** when you travel to Britain.

## 2 In der Gastfamilie (*Guest in a foreign family*)

→ Übungen ab S. 237

1. Musterlösung:
   a) May I / Is it OK if I phone my family?
   b) Shall I help you clear the table? / What shall I do with these dirty plates and glasses?
   c) Where can I wash my clothes? / Is it OK if I wash my clothes?
   d) May I go out with some of the other students this evening?
   e) Could you tell me where to catch the bus to the city centre? / Where can I catch the bus to the city centre?

**Bildquellenverzeichnis**
**Fotolia, New York:** 210. (Vincent); **Thinkstock, München:** 36.1 (prostooleh), 36.2 (monkeybusinessimages), 36.3 (Iscreativo), 36.4 (MarioGuti), 47.1 (AlexBrylov), 47.2 (maxximmm), 47.3 (Stockbyte), 47.4 (Ingram Publishing), 53.1 (TonyBaggett), 53.2 (Brockswood), 53.3 (Halfpoint), 53.4 (Hallgerd), 63.1 (monkeybusinessimages), 63.2 (Fuse), 63.3 (Marc Debnam), 63.4 (NeonShot), 78.1 (evgenyatamanenko), 78.2 (amana productions inc.), 78.3 (Flying Colours Ltd), 78.4 (Fuse), 78.5 (iZhenya), 78.6 (Thinkstock), 100.1 (Marc_Espolet), 100.2 (delmonte1977), 100.3 (Artyom Rudenko), 100.4 (unalozmen), 113.1 (Stacey Newman), 113.2 (Ryan McVay), 113.3 (Fuse), 113.4 (Dominic_Dahncke), 131.1 (monkeybusinessimages), 131.2 (BananaStock), 131.3 (oksun70), 147.1 (lovleah), 147.2 (moodboard), 147.3 (Irina_ Zholudeva), 156.1 (fotofritz16), 156.2 (DieBuben), 168. (CaronB), 175. (Russell102), 185. (thehague), 189.1 (kdshutterman), 189.2 (kaarsten), 189.3 (moodboard), 189.4 (Purestock), 189.5 (Wavebreakmedia Ltd), 189.6 (Ingram Publishing), 189.7 (EdnaM), 189.8 (bernie_photo), 201. (ViktorCap), 202. (Maridav), 208.1 (RyanKing999), 208.2 (ian35mm), 208.3 (Nickos), 208.4 (CBCK-Christine), 214.1 (niolox), 214.2 (Geshas), 214.3 (udra), 214.4 (MSPhotographic), 215. (MarcQuebec), 229. (simongurney), 231. (Brockswood)